**JEWISH-AMERICAN ARTISTS
AND THE HOLOCAUST**

Jewish-American Artists and the Holocaust

MATTHEW BAIGELL

Rutgers University Press
New Brunswick, New Jersey, and London

Library of Congress Cataloging-in-Publication Data
Baigell, Matthew.
    Jewish-American artists and the Holocaust / Matthew Baigell.
        p.   cm.
    Includes bibliographical references and index.
    ISBN 0-8135-2404-0 (alk. paper)
        1. Jewish artists—United States. 2. Holocaust, Jewish (1939–1945), in art.
    3. Art, American. 4. Art, Modern—20th century—United States.   I. Title.
N6538.J4B35 1997
704.9'499405318—dc21   96-39806
                                                                                                                              CIP

British Cataloging-in-Publication information available

Manufactured in the United States of America

For Lola Schwimmer Rewitz Mozes
Auschwitz Number A-14989
and for
Renee
Leah and Henry, Naomi and Greg
Max, Zachary, Tali, and those yet to come

CONTENTS

PREFACE

Over the last two decades, many, many Jewish-American artists all over the United States have turned to Jewish themes. No aspect of Jewish life and culture seems to have been ignored; subjects range from cabalistic mysticism to traditional images of Grandma lighting the Sabbath candles, and artists have used and explored all media and many modes of presentation.

Although I had intended to write a survey of this unprecedented outpouring of interest in Jewish heritage, memory, religion, and current experiences, it soon became obvious that among the subjects explored by the artists, one was the most popular and generated more emotion than all the others: That subject was the Holocaust. I soon realized that my survey would be skewed by the sheer size and emotional weight of the chapter or chapters on Holocaust art. I therefore decided to write a book devoted exclusively to images of the Holocaust by Jewish-American artists. My starting point would be the 1930s.

While I was preparing this study, art historian Ziva Amishai-Maisels of Hebrew University, Israel, brought out her large, encyclopedic work, *Depiction and Interpretation: The Influence of the Holocaust on the Visual Arts*, a study of Holocaust imagery from the 1930s through the early 1980s by artists around the world.[1] Rather than review much of the material covered in her book, I chose instead to concentrate more narrowly on the art of the last twenty years. Even with this contraction of my focus,

I decided to work only with Jewish-American artists because I was more interested in their responses to the Holocaust than in more generalized responses from the larger American art community.

In the last few years I corresponded with about eighty artists whose names I obtained from catalogs of exhibitions on Jewish themes, from museum curators, from a list of artists provided by the United States Holocaust Memorial Museum, from other artists, and from friends and relatives. Most artists responded to my initial letter and questionnaire, some did not, and some could not be located. I assume that there are dozens upon dozens more whom I did not contact among those who use Holocaust imagery. Monica Bohm-Duchen said immediately after the symposium held in conjunction with the exhibition she organized, *After Auschwitz,* which toured England in 1995, that even though she had spent four years preparing the exhibition, she had just heard the names and had seen slides of the work of several artists of whom she had been completely unaware.[2] So I regret very much not having been able to contact all those artists who use or have used Holocaust imagery and who remain unknown to me.

There were, however, a few artists whom I decided not to include in this study, either because their work did not lend itself to inclusion or their styles and sensibilities were formed abroad—in the latter instance, these include Samuel Bak in Europe and Israel, and Leonid Lamm in the former Soviet Union.

After collecting and collating the material, I made a few key decisions. First, I chose not to discriminate among those artists who have employed Holocaust imagery only once and those who use it regularly. Second, I did not impose an organization based on types of subject matter, since this seemed entirely too arbitrary. Instead, I allowed the flow of the text to proceed as the material seemed to warrant. Nor did I try to separate out aspects of theory, memory, and history. This does occur in books and articles on Holocaust literature and memorials as well as in movies. I found that doing so distanced me from, and inhibited my emotional and visceral responses to, the artists' works (let alone to the Holocaust itself), and caught me up instead in intellectual constructs which I felt violated the intentions of most, if not all, of the artists.

I owe debts of gratitude to Norman Kleeblatt, who a few years ago happily (for me) insisted that I look at aspects of American art within a Jewish context, and to his colleagues at the Jewish Museum, Susan Goodman, Susan Chevlowe, Mira Goldfarb Berkowitz, and Lisa Leavitt for providing access to their files; to Stephen Feinstein for sharing his immense knowledge of Holocaust materials with me; and to Donald Kuspit for his constant encouragement. I especially want to thank Leslie Mitchner for her initial enthusiasm and support for this project as well as Marilyn Campbell, both of the Rutgers University Press. Susan H. Llewellyn's editorial talents saved the manuscript from far too many stylistic infelicities. In addition I want to acknowledge Rabbi Bennett Miller for his acute sense of *tikkun olam* (repair of the world), and I also want to acknowledge Dr. Gerard Hellman, whose devotion to his profession has been an inspiration to me in mine. And, most important, I want to express my gratitude to Renee Baigell, whose ideas, as with everything I write, appear on virtually every page.

**JEWISH-AMERICAN ARTISTS
AND THE HOLOCAUST**

Children of Survivors— "Memorial Candles"

As I mentioned in the preface, during my research for this book I corresponded with some eighty Jewish-American artists. I was struck by the fact that the responses I received from children of survivors, written a half century after the Holocaust, indicate that their burden was and still is enormous—and different from that borne by those whose families were nor directly affected by the events of the 1940s. For example, Anna Bialobroda, aware of the Holocaust from childhood, has been "shouldering since then the deeply mutilating impact the Holocaust had on my parents" (fig. 21). Although her parents were able to tell her about their experiences (not all such parents were willing or able to do so), "the sense of loss was a silent omnipresence in our house."[1] Growing up with this knowledge; understanding that one's parents had had different experiences from the parents of one's friends; learning, as Art Spiegelman relates, while sleeping over at a friend's house, that not everybody's parents scream in the middle of the night; realizing that one might come to know the names of relatives but never see them, prompted author Arthur A. Cohen to call such children members of "the generation that bears the scar without the wound, sustaining memory without direct experience."[2]

In the generational chain, they are usually the firstborn after the Holocaust (Mindy Weisel [fig. 23] says that she was the first child born in Bergen-Belsen after it had been converted into a displaced persons camp) and the last to be directly linked to the lost European culture. They are truly a generation that looks backward and forward, and, because of that, various obligations have been thrust upon them. As Wendy Joy Kuppermann has said: "I bear witness. I inhabit the space of an altar, not as a burnt offering, but as a memorial candle lit at inception. Perhaps that is my original job description" (fig. 17).[3]

In Dina Waldi's study of children of survivors, she determined that quite often one of the children—most often a daughter—in a survivor family becomes the designated "memorial candle": the one "given the burden of participating in [the] parents' emotional world to a much greater extent than any of [the other siblings]." The child becomes the link with the past, the one who helps to preserve the past and the one who helps to negotiate the present and future. Generated by the vacuum left by the Holocaust, the role makes the "memorial candle" the one who takes on the responsibilities of the lost extended family, the one responsible for intergenerational continuity. As Waldi summarized, the message transmitted to this as well as to other siblings, who are not necessarily excused from their responsibilities, is:

> You are the continuing generation. Behind us are ruin and
> death and infinite emotional emptiness. It is your obligation and
> your privilege to maintain the nation, to reestablish the van-
> ished family, and to fill the enormous physical and emotional
> void left by the Holocaust.[4]

In whatever ways artists provide for their parents' needs, the obligation to do so enters their art and the ways they think about their art. It does not necessarily follow, however, that artists are "memorial candles" or even want to be considered in that way. But Weisel, for example, loves the concept and says that the key word is "responsible":

> As a survivor's child, I have felt this tremendous responsibility
> of not only expressing what my parents had endured in
> Auschwitz, but also to be the link to the old European customs,
> traditions, and elegance I was raised with. I tell my three
> daughters, "I can't let it die with me." It is exactly this desire to

translate my parents' emotional world into paintings that
prompted my doing *Paintings of the Holocaust* (1980), in which
I used my father's concentration camp number, A3146, on all
the works . . . , to the series I finished last year, *Lili, Let's
Dance* [to commemorate her mother's death in 1994].

On another occasion she said:

I don't think I was ever aware of how *obsessed* I really am with
my parents. . . . I knew that I lived my life so that I'd make them
happy. If I were on an airplane I didn't worry that if it went down
I should die, I'd worry how would they survive my death? I was
so important; I was the *first born.* I really took care of them.

It is telling that the terms she uses to describe her feelings—the
caring, the nurturing, even the need to be "the link to the old"—are also
characteristic of the parent-child relationship; it is as if the child has in
a sense become the parent, and is seeking to give back in another form
something of what was taken away.

The series *Paintings of the Holocaust* dealt with her feelings toward
her father. One work in the series, "Ovens" (in the collection of Yad
Vashem), was an attempt "to understand and express the tremendous
sadness and pain I felt over what my family had endured."[5] All the works
in this series have large internal borders that frame what seem like
charred remains of a conflagration. In these paintings Weisel would first
build up layers of light-colored paint, which were then overrun with black
pigment. The tension between beauty, represented by the lighter colors,
and destruction, represented by black pigment, is palpable and clearly
stands as a visual metaphor for the effects of the Holocaust on the lives
of innocent people.

As much as their art memorializes their parents' experiences, some artists have admitted that they create works to help contain
their own anxieties about those experiences. Kuppermann says that her
personal Holocaust "knows . . . no temporal distinctions. *That is the timeless core of the Second Generation experience*" [italics in original]. The literary historian Lawrence Langer has posted the concepts of "durational
time" and "chronological time," in relation to camp survivors. Durational
time refers to camp memories which remain forever present in the

minds of many if not all former prisoners. It is the time—camp time, frozen time—in which many still live, unable to put their experiences and memories behind them. "Chronological time" refers to the on-going time in which the rest of us live and in which survivors also live.[6] In an analogous manner, time for Kuppermann also collapses as the presence of her parents' Holocaust folds into her own.

Like other children of survivors, she was also "not merely traumatized . . . but in essence *possessed* by the demons of our parents' brutal and dehumanizing experiences." As a child she thought that all adults had numbers and letters on their arms, and that all adult conversation was about losses, roundups, and hunger. She had "absorbed an implacable nameless grief coupled with terror." So it is no wonder that for her "the Holocaust [remains] the single most important fact of my existence." A traumatizing trip to Poland with her parents in 1989 provoked in her the need not to ignore the Holocaust and run from her parent's experiences, but to overcome its impact. Her art, then, began and continues to function "as a vital therapeutic outlet and coping mechanism personally redemptive, although necessarily painful. It is an exorcism of demons."[7]

Grace Graupe-Pillard also acknowledges that her art serves a self-healing process (fig. 35). She says that the explorations of her family history in her Holocaust pieces are selfishly cathartic. "I use art to express my own dread and awe of the vagaries of the world I live in," in great measure brought about by the fact that she has been "impacted by my parents' experience of flight from the land of their birth."[8]

Visits by the artists to their parents' countries and/or hometowns —whether shocking, therapeutic, or merely emotion-filled—clearly have been an important goad to the making of art. While growing up, Elyse Klaidman heard countless stories about the war years but had been unable to integrate them into her feelings and her life. After traveling to Czechoslovakia in 1990 with her mother, Kitty Klaidman, she found herself finally able to use Holocaust imagery, as if a wellspring of images and emotions had been released. "I realized," she says, "that throughout the years, I had stored imagery in my mind. Some of what I confronted was eerily similar to what I had imagined and some was strikingly different." Immediately on returning home she began to investigate her family's past, painting portraits of surviving and deceased relatives and the places where her mother had been hidden, and then, after a short time, more generalized images pertaining to the Holocaust (fig. 15).[9]

Remembrance is important on at least two levels—the public and the private. Clearly the significance of the former needs no elaboration. The latter is consequential for these artists because it helps provide the individual with ways to explain his or her selfhood and preoccupations with Holocaust subject matter. Debbie Teicholz reveals much when she says:

> The Holocaust is the central event that was the turning point in my parents' life, the trauma of which was transferred to me. . . . I am a child of survivors, and it has defined me. . . . The persistence of the theme of the Holocaust in my work has evolved from my identification as a child of survivors and my compulsion to examine the personal effects of [this] on my life.

And, like other such artists, she reveals some anxiety—not having been a participant in her parents' experiences—over her inability to be certain if her work captures the qualities she seeks. Teicholz says that she wants to bear witness to a past in which she did not participate: "I wish to portray an aspect of memory which is not a memory, but remembering a memory, or a simulated memory."

This is more complicated than it sounds. First, it suggests an identification beyond empathy with her parents. And, second, it also suggests that Teicholz either can or would like to enter into that time frame where chronological time melts into durational time. Whether prompted by guilt, curiosity, a sense of responsibility, or other motivations, she wants deeply to understand—perhaps even experience vicariously—the past events in her parents' lives. As she says: "My identity was greatly influenced by a past from which I am once removed. My art bears witness to this feeling of displacement, of living in a time warp, where a flashback to the Holocaust takes place simultaneously with events of today" (fig. 16). The creation of works with this feature—the past embedded in the present—also serves, as with Kuppermann and Graupe-Pillard, as part of a spiritual healing process for the artist.[10]

Creating works about (or because of) one's parents' experiences does not make an artist a memorial candle. In fact, Pier Marton and Natan Nuchi do not want to be considered anything other than children of survivor parents. It is a question for them of designation, not of sympathy and understanding. Marton, for example, has said, "I am a witness to my parents, their wound is mine. . . . Knowing our parents had *almost* been killed many times, we grew up with a particular chill in our bones." He goes on, "Being the oldest child has affected me in terms of being the person who received the first, most of the burden and who feels responsible." Even though this might sound like the self-definition of a memorial candle, Marton regards that classification as too simplistic and trite. The issue is too complicated for him to allow easy classifications (fig. 41).[11]

Nuchi finds it problematic to connect personal psychology to art and the Holocaust. To emphasize the fact that he is a child of survivors, he says, is to emphasize his activity in psychological terms "and in a sense to turn it to an expression of a pathological condition rather than an expression of art." There is a difference, which he wants to keep apparent, between his "preoccupation" with the Holocaust as art and not as psychological expression, a difficult task at best (fig. 31).

He also feels that his father was many things other than a survivor, and so Nuchi's generational link is that of a partial memorial candle, he and his siblings being bequeathed different aspects of an emotional inheritance. He readily admits that as the child of a survivor family his interest in the Holocaust is not an arbitrary one, but, he says:

> I would like to emphasize that I regard the fact that my father was a survivor as secondary to many other reasons for dealing with the subject. . . . Such issues as the connection between the Holocaust's naked/nude figures and the history of figure painting, or the relation and contradiction between the Holocaust as subject matter for art and the rest of contemporary art, or the fact that for me, dwelling on the Holocaust provided an extreme vantage point from which I could consider the rest of culture more clearly. These seemed to me more urgent and important than the fact that I was the son of a survivor.[12]

These are serious issues of self-identity and of relationships with one's parents. Probably not all children of survivors would go as far as writer Julie Salamon, who said: "The Holocaust is so primal, especially for somebody whose parents are survivors. It's at the core of your being." But most would agree that "where our parents were unable to bear witness to the war, this has now become our duty."[13]

Before the War

Adolf Hitler became chancellor of Germany on January 30, 1933, and almost immediately the Left press in the United States began to publish cartoons hostile to his regime. But throughout the decade barely a handful of artists, whatever their political preferences, addressed the increasingly virulent outbreaks of anti-Semitism in Germany. The few who did include the Mexican Diego Rivera (1886–1957), and the Jewish Americans Ben Shahn (1898–1969) and Max Weber (1881–1961).

Rivera, one of the first to respond, included an anti-Semitic episode in a mural panel painted toward the end of 1933 in the didactic manner he used at that time. It was the "Hitler" panel, one of twenty-one that comprised his *Portrait of America*, made for the New Workers' School in New York City (fig. 1). Rivera supported himself while completing the panels with funds he had received for his ill-fated mural for the RCA Building in Rockefeller Center, *Man at the Crossroads Looking with Uncertainty but with Hope and High Vision to the Choosing of a Course Leading to a New and Better Future*, which was destroyed in 1933 because it included, among other scenes, a portrait of Lenin. The New Workers' School murals were destroyed in a fire in the 1960s.

The text accompanying these murals, written by the school's director, Bertram D. Wolfe, was probably the first extensive account of

Nazi atrocities written for an art publication in the United States.[1] In the panel Albert Einstein, the world's foremost Jewish scientist, appears in the lower left corner, a symbol of the German desire to eliminate from that country any critical thought. Standing next to Einstein is a tortured Jewish person "whose sin is in his blood." Next to him is a Christian woman with shaven head, who is paraded through the streets for endangering Aryan purity. She wears a sign around her neck: I HAVE GIVEN MYSELF TO A JEW. This particular episode was based on an actual event witnessed and reported by several American newspaper correspondents.[2] At the panel's edge, next to the woman, is a portrait of Hermann Göring, whom Wolfe called an insane dope addict. In the center of the panel, adjacent to Hitler's mouth, a sterilization operation takes place. Above Hitler's head, sadistic tortures are shown. A book burning takes place under Nazi flags.

With probably no newspaper or magazine photographs on which to ground his images, Rivera invented the scenes contained in the "Hitler" panel. Four years later, in 1937, Ben Shahn, with little more available visual documentation of the atrocities being carried out against German Jews, depicted two small, anti-Semitic episodes adjacent to each other in his mural for Jersey Homesteads (now Roosevelt), a town in central New Jersey newly established by the Resettlement Administration, primarily for Jewish garment workers in the International Ladies' Garment Workers Union. (The Resettlement Administration, a unit of the Farm Security Administration, was a part of President Franklin Roosevelt's New Deal programs to revitalize the American economy.) Shahn, who had worked with Rivera on the Rockefeller Center project, created a mural that shows immigrants, led by Einstein, arriving at Ellis Island, passing the coffins of Nicola Sacco and Bartolomeo Vanzetti, the Italian anarchists executed in 1927 for the murder of an armored car guard; working in sweatshops; becoming union members; and, through education and enlightened union leadership, moving from unhealthy ghettos to rural towns such as Roosevelt.

Various changes were made in the preliminary designs before Shahn began the mural in true fresco. Initially the work was conceived as a narrative of life in a Russian ghetto—the difficulties encountered there, which included pogroms—and then the immigration to the United States. Toward the side of a study for the mural, a Jewish worker stands with two children on a divided pathway. One road leads to

Palestine and the other to a cooperative rural community in the United States: The choice is, in effect, to remain Jewish or become American. The worker must decide quickly because, as Shahn wrote in the spring of 1936, "over him hangs a dark reddish cloud in which the horrors of Jewish persecution in Hitler Germany are shown. The cloud hangs low with a sense of imminence."[3] In a subsequent design for the upper-left-hand corner of the mural, where the narrative would begin, Shahn planned to show a riot taking place, overlaid by coffins containing the bodies of African Americans. For the mural itself, however, Shahn Americanized his subject matter, focusing on the United States as a safe haven for Jews, but he indicated that political oppression existed here, as well. Einstein, who was not included in early studies, now leads the way into this country. Behind the coffins of Sacco and Vanzetti, Shahn now included a German in uniform holding a sign that says GERMANS, DEFEND YOURSELVES: DON'T BUY FROM JEWS (in German) (fig. 2). Immediately to the left a sign, pasted over the wall plaque of a Dr. I. Koch, states, ATTENTION JEWS: VISIT FORBIDDEN.[4] By 1937 events of this type had been reported regularly in the American press.

In 1938 Max Weber, who had worked with Jewish subject matter for the previous twenty years, addressed, if obliquely, the plight of Jews in Central Europe. Reminiscing in the late 1950s, he recalled how he came to paint *Whither Now?*:

> When I heard of Hitler (I knew a Hitler was coming several years before anybody heard the name) and when I heard that he was beginning to break the Jewish shops in Berlin and all that, I could see what an anti-Semite could do when he's bloodthirsty and fanatic and crazy. I said, "Look, I'm doing abstract art. Nobody is bothering me. Nobody is shattering my windows, my house. Oh, where are the people going to go now? What are these Jewish people in Germany going to do? And [Hitler] is awakening an anti-Semitism that is going to be ruinous." So I said, "Where to?" And I painted a large canvas of two Jews called "Whither Now?"[5]

Perhaps Weber painted this work in immediate response to Kristallnacht ("crystal night," from the broken glass that was its most memorable sound and image), the name since designated to commemorate the burning and destruction of synagogues, the smashing and looting of Jewish businesses, and the physical assaults on Jews on the night of November 9, 1938. In any event the left-hand figure in the painting is sightless, as if to suggest that the future cannot be predicted with any certainty. Further, the physical insubstantiality of the figures also suggests that the world these two men have inhabited has begun to vanish, that their very incorporeality already embodies the situation in which European Jews would soon find themselves.[6] Weber was nothing if not prescient: Early in the next year, 1939, Hitler said that a European war would lead to "the destruction of the Jewish race in Europe."[7]

By the late 1930s other American artists, including Benjamin Kopman, Moses Soyer, William Gropper, Abraham Harriton, as well as Weber, painted scenes of refugees often trudging across bleak landscapes. Some of these scenes, however, might just as easily be imaginary depictions of refugees fleeing from battles during the Spanish Civil War as of groups of East Europeans moving from community to community.[8] No doubt these and other artists often discussed the European situation, but they did not develop a subject matter to deal with it beyond such generalized images. Nor did they refer to it often in their work.

It was not as if they were unaware, however. In the art press, for example, there were several references to Hitler's activities, to his attacks on Jews, on non-Aryan and non-German culture, and on artistic freedom. *Art Digest,* then the art magazine of record, cited passages of Hitler's speech, condemning foreign culture and its harmful effects on German society, when he assumed the chancellorship in 1933. In its issue for November 1 of that year, one could read that Hitler banned German-Jewish artists from entering Pittsburgh's annual Carnegie International Exhibition. Two years later the magazine printed a report that all non-Aryan art dealers in Germany had had to close their galleries. And at the opening of the *Haus der Kunst* (House of German Art) in Munich in July 1937, the magazine recorded Hitler's increasingly outspoken attacks on Jews.[9] Similar articles could also be found in the daily press and various magazines.

Some explanations can be offered for the relative lack of interest in such subject matter. Europe was, in the 1930s, an ocean away. For artists living outside New York City, and those associated with American Scene painting, the most popular art movement of the time, primacy was given to subject matter based on American history, customs, and current events. One would not expect them to become involved with European Jewish concerns. And besides, newspaper reports about anti-Semitic events were not always as clear as they might have been. Editors, skeptical about reports of persecution, were fearful of being duped once again by anti-German propaganda as they had been in the years before the United States entered the World War I in 1917. Evidently they tended to downplay, or simply did not believe, their correspondents' dispatches.[10]

Nor was the American motion picture industry very responsive during the 1930s. Far from trying to galvanize public opinion, it hardly even responded to the rise of Nazism. Distributors booked films into German cinemas until America's entry into the war and had no intention of losing their German accounts. The Production Code, which studios were only too happy to honor in this instance, recommended that the Jewish presence in films be minimized as much as possible. This lasted right though the war. And during the war years, the *Government Information Manual for the Motion Picture Industry* suggested that the problems of a single group should not divert attention from the war effort. With the exception of Charlie Chaplin's *The Great Dictator,* which appeared in 1940, "no explicit presentation of the Jewish catastrophe" was made until 1959, with the production of the movie version of *The Diary of Anne Frank.*[11]

The desire to suppress Jewish issues also grew from the fears of Jewish studio owners that gentiles would blame Jews for the world's problems and thus contribute to the spread of anti-Semitism in the United States. This fear was borne out by several contemporary studies that documented levels of American anti-Semitism. For example, after Kristallnacht, the percentage of Americans who would have allowed increased German-Jewish immigration to this country rose from 17 to only 21 percent. A survey taken in 1938 reported that about 60 percent of those polled thought that Jews had brought persecution on themselves. Surveys conducted between 1938 and 1941 showed that up to 50 percent of the public believed that Jews had too much power. During that three-year period, in spite of constant press reports concerning the fate of European Jewry, only 5 percent thought that Jews had grown more patriotic. In another poll about 25 percent of the respondents felt that Jews were a menace to the United States. These figures did not reflect the kind of political and social climate in which Jewish-Americans would insist, even if they felt the need, on calling attention to the plight of their coreligionists abroad.[12]

During the 1930s the art world itself was not free of open anti-Semitism. For example, in a book surveying modern art, the xenophobe and anti-Semite Thomas Craven, the most popular and most powerful art critic during that decade, referred to Alfred Stieglitz (1864–1946), the great photographer and early proselytizer of modern art, as "a Hoboken Jew without knowledge of, or interest in, the historical American background," and a figure who was "hardly equipped for the leadership of a genuine American expression."[13] To be sure, Craven attacked virtually all popular artists whose names did not sound Anglo-Saxon, but he was especially vitriolic in reference to Stieglitz.

Craven's good friend Thomas Hart Benton (1889–1975), the major and most visible American Scene painter during the 1930s, was no friend to the Jews through the middle years of that decade. A resident of New York City until 1935, when he moved to Kansas City, he argued publicly and in print with New York–based artists, mostly about politics and about their lack of knowledge and understanding of the American environment. But a subtext of his excoriations was that he seemed not to be able to keep separate in his mind distinctions between Jewish and left-wing artists and, in effect, damned both in the same breath for not being quite American enough.[14]

There were obviously other instances of covert and overt anti-Semitism in the art and literary fields. One might imagine that left-leaning artists, particularly Jewish-American ones, would have responded more openly to such provocations. It is true that the artist Moses Soyer (1899–1975), exasperated by the American Scene paintings on view at the 1935 Whitney Museum Biennial, warned artists against being "misled by the chauvinism of the 'Paint America' slogan. Yes," he said, "paint America, but with your eyes open. Do not glorify Main Street. Paint it as it is—mean, dirty, avaricious. Self-glorification is artistic suicide. Witness Nazi Germany."[15]

Soyer's outburst was prompted, no doubt, by the treatment of Jews in Germany. But another factor comes into play as well. Artists of both Soyer's generation and the following one were immigrants or the children of immigrants. They wanted to escape the ghetto to become Americans—not Middle Western Americans, but Americans with legitimate American experiences of their own. Writers such Craven and Benton denied the validity of their experiences, relegating them forever to the position of outsider or foreigner, particularly Jewish foreigner. In Soyer's mind the attitudes expressed by these figures were not too distant from those expressed by Hitler and, by 1935, already being acted on in Germany. It is not too far-fetched to imagine that Craven and Benton were terrifying figures because of what they potentially represented to Jewish Americans—the rise of an American fascism.

But Soyer's outburst nonetheless seems to have been the exception rather than the rule among Jewish-American artists. This is not so surprising when one considers the involvement of the Communist Party in art matters during the 1930s. Its influence on these artists to repress any Jewish expression coincided with the artists' own desires to escape their Jewish backgrounds for the larger American context. This is not the place to discuss who was or was not a party member, or the extent to which the party influenced individual artists. But it is clear that the party was a presence in the lives of many Jewish-American artists. Some were members, some were close followers, and the party did control such major organizations as the John Reed clubs (1929–1935) and the American Artists' Congress (1936–1942), as well as various magazines and newspapers that were important to the artists.

The Communist Party, especially during its so-called third period, from roughly 1928 to 1933, opposed ethnic and religious particularism for its greater task of proletarianizing the masses. During these years it especially "attacked organized religion and ethnic separation," as well as the group loyalties of Jews, Finns, and Slavs.[16] As a result, party-line writers and artists attacked Jewish institutions, business interests, and the rabbinate in articles and cartoons. Nazi assaults on the Jews, then, although motivated by anti-Semitism, were also considered to be the outcome of problems contained within late capitalism. So Moses Soyer's coupling of American Scene painting with Nazi Germany may well have reflected this particular Communist interpretation of Hitler's actions and the Communist concern for the spread of fascism to the United States, as it may have mirrored Soyer's own concerns for Jewish people in Germany. That is, Soyer and others may have felt a greater responsibility to Communist policies than to helping the Jews of Germany. And so the art world's relative silence to German anti-Semitism, which was considered less a problem of racial hatred than an economic one.

It is interesting to note here that since many Yiddish- and foreign-language-speaking Jews were politically left of center, the central committee of the American Communist Party established a Jewish bureau in order to reach what it hoped was a receptive audience. The justification for this particularist approach by a universalist organization was to teach Yiddish-speaking workers to accept Communism and reject Jewish culture, which, led by business and religious interests, was trying to overwhelm and control the Jewish working classes. So concerned was the party to organize the Jewish masses that when it established the John Reed clubs to proletarianize artists and writers, it also established a Jewish equivalent, the Proletpen (*allgemeine proletarische schreiber-organizazia*). That many members of the John Reed clubs were also Jewish did not seem to matter.[17]

During these years Communists also equated American governmental policies with fascism. As Earl Browder, general secretary of the American Communist Party from 1934 to 1945, declared, the New Deal is "not developed fascism. But in political essence and direction it is the same as Hitler's program." Therefore, the answer Bertram Wolfe gave when asked if he would oppose efforts to stop Hitler should he try to conquer Europe might well have reflected the thoughts of many Jewish Americans on the Left. Wolfe said that such speculation was improbable, since capitalists were the same everywhere. Only the working class could overthrow the capitalists.[18] His answer implied that it was far more important to overthrow fascism/capitalism than to become involved with a particularist group such as the Jews.

Soviet policy changed in 1935 with the institution of the Popular Front. Cooperation with any group or person who opposed the fascist powers—Germany, Italy, Japan—replaced the immediate desire to overthrow capitalism. American democratic policies were now tolerated, and Jewish culture was rehabilitated. Anti-Semitism was specifically addressed at the Communist-sponsored International Conference Against Anti-Semitism and Racial Hatred, held in Paris in 1936. A call urging "the formation of a world Yiddish cultural congress to defend modern Yiddish culture against Hitlerism" was soon followed by the formation of the World Alliance of Jewish Culture (Yiddisher Kultur Farband [YKUF]). At the first art exhibition of the American branch in 1938, 102 artists, both Jewish and non-Jewish, participated. Their styles ranged from abstract to realistic; the message of the organizers was that Jewish creativity existed in a time of persecution.[19] It was acceptable to be Jewish again and to say as much. But even so, it may have been easier for many Jewish-American artists to remain anti-German than to become pro-Jewish—at least in public. This may help to explain Ben Shahn's astonishing comment, as reported by his wife, the artist Bernarda Bryson, that Shahn preferred to generalize subject matter concerned with war, even after 1945, rather than indulge in "ethnic self-pity."[20]

The War

Even artists who were not involved in left politics still would have found it difficult to make works of art explicitly about German anti-Semitism. Leaders of the Jewish community did not, or could not, mobilize public opinion in ways they can today. The press, at least outside New York City, did not emphasize what by 1942 had become Germany's plan to murder all European Jews. As Deborah Lipstadt has recorded in her book on the press's behavior, "Over the course of the years to 1945, the details would multiply, but the doubts would never be completely erased." Indeed, the press tended to ignore or minimize the situation. American anti-Semitism was still so strong during the war years that surveys taken between 1940 and 1946 revealed "that Jews were almost constantly seen as a greater menace to the welfare of the United States than were any other national, religious, or racial group," including, according to one poll in 1944, Germans or Japanese. Even the Office of War Information (OWI), for which Ben Shahn worked during the war years, tried to limit the publication of Jewish atrocity stories because it did not want the public to think that the Germans were hostile only to Jewish people. Rather, OWI policy held that their fate was to be considered coequal with that of other combatants and civilians.[1]

Most Jewish Americans, of course, knew what was happening. I knew in 1943, although I was barely ten years old. On December 2, 1942, some half million Jewish people in New York City stopped work for ten minutes as a form of protest, and some radio stations observed a two-minute period of silence that afternoon. A pageant, one of several memorial ceremonies, was held the following March in Madison Square Garden, dedicated to the two million Jews killed that year. And in April 1944, on the first anniversary of the Warsaw Ghetto uprising, more than thirty thousand Jewish Americans gathered at City Hall in New York to hear the mayor and others honor the memories of those who had died.[2]

Yet Jewish-American artists barely responded in their work or in written or verbal statements. The reasons are not difficult to imagine. Very few wanted to be labeled "a Jewish artist." In calling attention to his or her Jewishness, such an artist might be attacked or neglected and be likely to lose his or her supportive public. As awareness of the enormity of the situation grew, artists no doubt also had difficulty in visually imagining what was taking place and therefore could not eas-ily formulate pictorial responses. Even combatants who saw the camps immediately after the war "could not grasp what they were seeing"— both the sights they actually saw and the full intentions of the Germans.[3] As a result many artists probably wanted to dissociate themselves from the situation out of a sense of fear, incomprehension, and a desire to leave the European world behind.

To say all this in a few quick words clearly does not record the way Jewish Americans felt. People of my parents' generation, when talking about the war, even decades later, invariably mentioned their profound despair, their sense of utter helplessness, and their apprehensiveness about anti-Semitism in this country. In response to this last point, I and every-body I knew learned that however one felt or acted among one's own, to the world one should appear as non-Jewish as possible. Precisely where the internalized mainstream view of oneself as the "bad other" shaded into acceptable means of helping oneself remained a moot question— as did the issue of when self-hatred blended into self-protection. As in the old joke, it was not easy being Jewish—and it was more difficult try-ing not to be Jewish.

Even the most articulate became inarticulate. Through the 1940s and well into the 1950s, Jewish intellectuals and literary figures had trouble facing the Holocaust directly. The reasons vary, but all center on a few basic notions: fear of anti-Semitism; embarrassment about being

Jewish; the desire not to identify as Jewish in a parochial sense, which is not the same thing; the desire to identify as American; and the inability to comprehend the murder of six million people. (In 1995 I attended a memorial service in which each of six people held one candle, each candle representing one million people, a sight that—although understandable on one level—is still totally incomprehensible on another.)

The presence of 176,000 survivors who immigrated to this country and Canada between 1946 and 1953 evidently did little to focus attention or to prompt writers to express themselves in print about the events of the war. Figures such as literary critics Lionel Trilling and Irving Howe, social scientist Daniel Bell, psychologist Erik Erikson, religious philosopher Will Herberg, and art critics Harold Rosenberg and Clement Greenberg did not, or could not, indicate in their writings the impact these events must have had on them. As Irving Howe recalled in his autobiographical memoir, *A Margin of Hope,* it was difficult to make any kind of response. There were no received categories of thought to contain them, no metaphors to invoke. The break in the logical development in Western history was too vast to incorporate into one's thoughts. Novelists as well tended to ignore the Holocaust. "Fear of American anti-semitism and horror at a more virulent German strain contributed to a bland Jewish-American fiction that extolled sameness, brotherhood, and caution," was the way literary historian Dorothy Bilik described such immediately postwar work. Another historian, Edward Alexander, noted that "the imagination of most American Jewish writers was not effectively touched by the Holocaust either during its occurrence or for over two decades afterward."[4]

I do not take Bilik's and Alexander's observations to be criticisms, but rather realizations that the Holocaust was, for Jews everywhere, a primal injury. The more one learned about what occurred in the camps and the ghettos, the more foreign they became even to one's wildest imaginings. The disjunctions and disruptions between the events of the Holocaust and one's imaginative responses were simply too enormous to bridge easily. How was one to base an art on inconceivable experiences?

The kinds of statements that could be made decades after the war, when the full impact of the Holocaust had sunk in and been internalized by artists, would probably have left people numb in the late 1940s and 1950s. Four such statements will suffice.

Auschwitz survivor Primo Levi wrote that despite all subsequent mass killings:

> The Nazi concentration camp system still remains a unicum, both in its extent and its quality. At no other place or time has one seen a phenomenon so unexpected and so complex: never have so many human lives been extinguished in so short a time, and with so lucid a combination of technological ingenuity, fanaticism, and cruelty.

Sociologist Zygmunt Bauman, in his study of the unfortunate conjunction of anti-Semitism and the modern technological state's ability to murder so many people so rapidly, said:

> In virtually every one of its many aspects, it [the Holocaust] stands alone and bears no meaningful comparison with other massacres, however gory, visited upon groups previously defined as foreign, hostile, or dangerous.

But the thought that was probably least acceptable to the Jewish-American community might have been this one:

> The Holocaust was Nazi Germany's planned total destruction of the Jewish people and the actual murder of nearly six million of them. . . . The Nazis had intended destruction of the Jews to be total: they were to have been removed from history and memory.

That is, Jewish history and memory were to disappear, but, as Holocaust historian James E. Young has pointed out, Hitler had planned to "remember" Jews in his own way.

> By eradicating the Jewish *type* of memory, the Nazis would also have destroyed the possibility of regeneration through memory that has marked Jewish experience.[5]

However difficult it was to verbalize or visualize, internally or externally, one's feelings about the Holocaust itself, other related factors inhibited open discourse and expression of feelings about the event. Identification with the victims could only reinforce one's sense of Jewishness and the low esteem in which Jews were presumably held by the majority culture. In this country, where so many Jews had or were trying to acculturate or assimilate, negative values could reduce one's sense of self-identity and self-worth and might possibly lead to feelings of self-hatred.

This, in turn, might call into consideration the question of whether there was a center, a meaningful core, to any kind of Jewish-American identity.[6] Such important issues as the suburbanization of Jewish culture, the desire to leave behind Jewish parochialism and ethnic identity in order to find fulfillment in such American values as individual autonomy and personal accomplishment, the loss of the old idea of community, and the desire to forget the experiences of the war—often discussed in the pages of Jewish journals—all contributed to the deflection of interest in the Holocaust and to any great desire to express it in art. And among many of those on the political Left, the universalist-humanist dream that suppressed the truths of anti-Semitism and the uniqueness of the Holocaust in modern history was still a significant factor. In short, hardly anybody wanted to walk through life looking backward at a particularly tragic moment in Jewish history.[7]

To a greater or lesser degree, these thoughts engaged Jewish Americans all over the country no less than they did the so-called New York intellectuals, which included Clement Greenberg and Harold Rosenberg, two of the most powerful art critics of the period, and the artists associated with them, artists who became abstract expressionists. For example, in a symposium conducted by the magazine the *Contemporary Jewish Record,* on American literature and Jewish-American writers, Greenberg stated that he had "no more conscious position toward his Jewish heritage than the average American Jew—which is to say, hardly any." Whatever Jewish identity and qualities he possessed came to him informally, "mostly through mother's milk and the habits and talk of the family." He did not deny having some Jewish consciousness, but it was not very important to him. Like other New York figures, he wanted to become a cosmopolitan, a member of a worldwide community, rather than remain confined by his heritage—which, he thought, could not sustain serious intellectual or artistic development.

He believed that one must create one's own identity, and he also believed that the Jew-as-outsider, as an alienated being in an alienating world, was representative of the modern condition. In this regard the Jew became a type of everyman. In commenting on the plight of Jewish writers (and, by extension, Jewish artists), he said that it "becomes like every other plight today, a version of the alienation of man under capitalism; all plights merge, and that of the Jew has become less particular because it turns more and more into an intensified expression of a general one." Consequently, according to Greenberg, the Jewish writer is well situated to explore the modern condition because of his or her marginality, but not the source of his or her marginality—his or her Jewishness.[8]

Greenberg's position had not changed by 1950, when artists such as Mark Rothko, Adolph Gottlieb, Barnett Newman, and Seymour Lipton had already developed their mature styles. In an article entitled "Self-Hatred and Jewish Chauvinism," Greenberg summed up his attitude toward Judaism.[9] After considering Jewish self-hatred as a function of an underprivileged group's frustration at not being accepted by the majority culture because the former can never be fully emancipated from its origins (p. 426), he discussed Jewish chauvinism in what can only be described as outrageous terms. Writing two years after the founding of the State of Israel and five years after the end of World War II, Greenberg equated Jewish and German nationalism, since both were "born of a history of humiliation and defeat, and required a sharp blow or succession of blows in order to be awakened to action" (p. 428). The defeat of the various German states by Napoleon was balanced out in Greenberg's mind by pogroms and anti-Semitism, and he then proceeded to say that the Holocaust "was the equivalent (and much, much more) of what the 1918 defeat was for Germany" (p. 428). Even with the qualifying "and much, much more," one still blanches at Greenberg's preposterous equation.

Greenberg admitted that even though he was opposed to Jewish chauvinism and nationalism, he could readily understand how Jewish history might justify what he termed "Jewish national selfishness." In what has to be a classic instance of turning the other cheek (or a classic expression of intense Jewish self-hatred), he wrote:

> Those of us who are sick of Europe after Auschwitz and want to have nothing more to do with Gentiles have a right for the moment to indulge our feelings, if only to recover from trauma. But humanity in general is still the highest value and not all Gentiles are anti-Semites. Self-pity turned a good many Germans into swine, and it can do the same to others. . . . No mat-

ter how necessary it may be to indulge our feelings about
Auschwitz, we can do so only temporarily and privately; we
certainly cannot let them determine Jewish policy either in
Israel or outside it. (p. 429)

After presumably developing the requisite self-control to hide
his feelings so as not to rile the rest of the world, Greenberg offered
no real conclusion about how a Jewish person is supposed to think,
feel, or act about his or her sense of Judaism except in the most general terms. And he admitted it. He felt that an obligation to Jewish survival and to the Jewish community should be "personal and
spontaneous . . . , natural . . . not legislated . . . by ideology" (p. 432).
Jews will remain Jewish, he held, however assimilated they might
become, "as long as Jewishness remains essential to our sense of our
individual selves, as long as it is the truth about our individual selves"
(p. 433). Whatever that might mean. In this conclusion, which borders
on acceptance of the anti-Semitic notion that there is something inher-
ently or biologically—and therefore unacceptably—Jewish, Greenberg
clearly wrote as somebody who had no interest in the Jewish community and who wanted to forget the Holocaust as quickly as possible.

His position clearly affected his art criticism. Best known as a
formalist who held that each medium radically critiques its means of presentation, Greenberg believed, for example, that painting was about line,
shape, and color, and not about narrative content. His concern was for
aesthetics rather than for environment, place, or heritage. As one of the
most powerful critics of the 1950s, his views could not have been very
encouraging to those artists who might have wanted to commemorate
the Holocaust in their work, or even to find in formalism a mode of
response that might allow consideration of one of the major events, if
not the major event, of the twentieth century. By the elimination of
narrative traces, of all historical and contemporary references, such
artists might be pure in a Greenbergian sense, but they would also be
completing Hitler's task in that there would be no pictorial remembering
of the Holocaust. For Greenberg himself it would seem that in his insis-
tence on an ahistorical approach to picture making (except in the sense
of a continued critique of paint handling), he was removing himself as
much as possible from history, from his own ethnic roots, and reinventing
himself as an international cosmopolitan.

Harold Rosenberg, the other leading Jewish art critic of the 1950s, was more concerned with the notion of the Jew as the typical alienated modern person who aims to reinvent him- or herself as autonomous. More openly Jewish than Greenberg in his writings, Rosenberg championed art as a means to self-definition, as a way to find one's authentic self. He conflated the question of self-identity with Jewish identity by insisting that both were twentieth-century problems. So Jewish artists, like others, rather than conform to any past models, had by the 1950s begun "to assert their individual relation to art in an independent and personal way." As such, in that they were engaged in the act of creation as individuals rather than as members of a group, they were involved in "a profound expression" that was also a way of contributing to a genuine American art.[10] By finding the basis of art making in existentialist activity, Rosenberg neatly sidestepped any question of confronting the Holocaust in art, of the artist bringing an agenda to his or her art or, in the instance of Jewish American artists, of wanting to identify themselves as Jews through their art. Indeed, it would seem that the artist should be bereft of everything on which to build an identity but his or her essential personality. Like Greenberg, Rosenberg, too, appeared to want to leave behind the parochial world of Jewish culture, history, and heritage.

There is no way, of course, to determine the precise influence of these critics on Jewish-American artists. Rather, their example reflected a climate of opinion in the 1940s and 1950s that inhibited artists from proclaiming their Jewishness as a positive force in their lives and from responding to the Holocaust too loudly or insistently. On the other hand, there were and still are artists who found in the attitudes of Greenberg and Rosenberg justification for their own religious and artistic interests. Today, for example, several artists whom I contacted stated that their Jewish heritage had no influence on their artistic outlook, and that there was nothing Jewish in their work. Others indicated that they had been influenced to some extent by Jewish social values even as they rejected the religious aspects of Judaism. This particular configuration of responses ranged from outright rejection to partial tolerance of the respondents' Jewish heritage. Greenberg might have agreed that there was nothing to get excited about in this particular matter.

Several artists of Greenberg's generation would probably have had similar reactions. Adolph Gottlieb (1903–1974), for instance, created works for synagogues, most notably the curtain for the ark housing the Torah scrolls for Congregation B'nai Israel in Millburn, New Jersey, in 1950–1951. But Gottlieb rejected the notion that he was a Jewish artist. "The idea of being a so-called Jewish artist is like being a professional Jew," he said. "I think art is international and should transcend any racial, ethnic, or religious or national boundaries." For the curtain he was much more interested in the work's meaning through its overall design rather than through the particular symbols he used—which in any event did not lend themselves to a continuous narrative.[11] Seymour Lipton (1903–1986) said in regard to the sculptures he made for synagogues: "I don't practice the formal credo of Judaism, although I am deeply aware of my position as a Jew, both nostalgically, as to my parents, and politically, as one of a minority group." About his sculpture for synagogues, he felt that he solved certain formal and symbolic ideas and engaged in themes congruent with his attitudes.[12]

Jack Levine (born in 1915), who has explored Jewish subject matter since 1939, is less deracinated than were Gottlieb or Lipton. Yet, he revealed a similar ambivalence about his Jewishness when he explained that his father's death "started me on the path of painting these Jewish sages [for example, King David in 1940, King Solomon in 1941]. It was his religion, not mine." Of similar works that he made in the 1950s, he said: "I haven't gone into Judaica out of some sort of religious piety."[13] If anyone questioned Levine's religious piety or why he felt it necessary to defend himself, his comment does point to the general condition of being embarrassed by being a minority person in this country. And Leonard Baskin (b. 1922), while ruminating on his images of crows, said that he thought of those birds as "outcasts, not socially tasteful or acceptable. Maybe they are kind of a model for Blacks, Jews, Puerto Ricans, and everyone else who gets trapped in life. As a Jew, I have never had a bad experience, but I identify as a Jew, I feel very Jewish, very Yiddish, particularly, and so I think those crows in some sense are an expression of that."[14]

In the years just after the war, artistic references among these artists tended to be oblique rather than direct both in regard to their sense of Jewishness and to the Holocaust. As Jacob Landau (born in 1917) has acknowledged while reminiscing about those years, the Holocaust was surely one of the major events of the century, perhaps even of the millennium, but it was impossible to work directly with the raw visual data of the documentary photographs or to imagine similar scenes of the artist's own invention. He and others needed distance so as not to make works that were mawkish, vicious, or violent. The use of metaphor, he believes, seemed the only reasonable way to make art out of incredible horror.[15]

Of the artists most closely associated with Greenberg and Rosenberg—figures such as Lipton, Rothko, and Newman—it needs to be reiterated that they did not openly refer to the Holocaust, and that only Newman seems to have actively read Jewish texts at that time (as I will discuss later). Although my feeling is that, like Greenberg and Rosenberg, they were uncomfortable with their Jewishness, at the same time, it is easy for me to imagine that they were profoundly shaken and troubled by the Holocaust. In short, they were as conflicted and as tied up in emotional knots as anybody else from that generation who knew where he or she came from and who wanted to arrive at another place.

Lipton sculpted biblical and patriarchal figures in the early 1940s. His *Let My People Go* (1942) is a bust of a bearded man who wears over his head a prayer shawl that swoops down around his shoulders to become powerful forearms and hands. It is an image of defiance.[16] What might have been a graphic or realistic response to the European situation was deflected into an image of a biblical or at least a patriarchal figure. (This kind of imagery is discussed later in this chapter with the works of Ben-Zion.)

By 1945 Lipton had begun to explore a different kind of subject matter, which might have been influenced as much by the publication of photographs of concentration camp scenes as by the growing criticism of propagandistic paintings characteristic of the 1930s. As art historian Cecile Whiting has explained, art capable of making a "timeless statement" stood a better chance of escaping damnation as topical propaganda than did obvious, realistic pieces.[17]

Lipton's images were based on pre-Columbian death ritual sculptures, images of Moloch, and other sources that suggest violence or the possibility of violence. His work sprouted spikes that might impale, and contours developed jagged edges. Textures roughened. These qualities "became important to me," he said, "in terms of the hidden destructive forces below the surface of man." He explained that "thorns, bones (ancient and modern), sharp tensions, tusks, teeth, and harsh forms develop and grow together in varying ways as new beings of sculptural existence evoking images and moods of the primordial insides of man." Elucidating the way his work developed after 1945, he said that "the drive was toward finding sculptural structures that stemmed from the deep animal makeup of man's being. . . . The ferocity in these works relates to the biologic reality in man. . . . They are tragic statements on the condition of man, thereby ironically implying a courage to encompass evil, indifference, and dissonance in the world of man." And, finally, of his *Exodus* series of the late 1940s, he wrote that the individual pieces were "part of a tragic mood of history and reality that has always concerned me. . . . It is possible that Israeli history and emergence entered. I don't really know."[18]

In this series Lipton might just as easily have conveyed a happier mood, one of deliverance and freedom, of the biblical flight from Egypt, but the tragic mood Lipton sought instead must have been wrapped around his thoughts about the war years, for it is difficult to imagine such language growing from anything other than his responses to both the war and the Holocaust.

A sense of the tragic must also have inhabited the minds of other artists during the war years and immediately after. Rothko and Gottlieb, in the now famous and often cited letter they sent to Edward Alden Jewell, an art critic of the *New York Times*, in June 1943 (in response to an exhibition review he had written), explaining the nature of their art, asserted that "only that subject matter is *valid which is tragic and timeless*," certainly an appropriate choice for Jewish artists anywhere at that time.[19] But rather than create works directly related to the Holocaust, they found, especially in Friedrich Nietzsche's *The Birth of Tragedy*, a way to universalize their concerns and content. Rothko, like Nietzsche, saw in Greek tragedy a way to confront death and mortality, and it is in part for this reason that he and Gottlieb professed in their letter "a spiritual kinship with primitive and archaic art." As Nietzsche suggested, after humans begin to recognize their terror of death, "art [Greek tragedy] appears as a saving sorceress, expert at healing. She alone knows how to turn these nauseous thoughts about the horror or absurdity of existence into notions with which one can live."[20]

So Rothko's *The Omen of the Eagle* (1942), for example, refers to events in Aeschylus's *Oresteia*, the story of the House of Atreus. The painting includes the heads of two eagles, which Anna Chave, one of

Rothko's biographers, associates with Agamemnon and Menelaus, the warrior brothers. The former's children referred to themselves as "the eagle's brood" and, after Agamemnon was murdered, "the orphaned children of the eagle father." But eagles are also the national emblems of Germany and the United States, a connection Rothko may have been aware of. The painting may have been concerned with war not as a specific event, but as an assault on life and as a primal aggression, particularly against children.[21]

Like Lipton, Rothko found the activities of warfare and murder to be qualities inherent in humans, biological facts turned into social actions. As Rothko said during a radio broadcast in 1943,

> If our titles [both his and Gottlieb's] recall the known myths of antiquity, we have used them . . . because they are eternal symbols upon which we must fall back to express basic psychological ideas. . . . Those who think that the world today is more gentle and graceful than the primeval and predatory passions from which these myths spring, are either not aware of reality or do not wish to see it in art.

Gottlieb, who also took part in the broadcast, responded more explicitly to the cataclysm then overwhelming Europe.

> That these demonic and brutal images fascinate us today, is not because they are exotic, nor do they make us nostalgic for a past which seems enchanting because of its remoteness. . . . If we profess a kinship to the art of primitive men, it is because the feelings they expressed have a particular pertinence today. In times of violence, personal predilections for niceties of color and form seem irrelevant. All primitive expression reveals the constant awareness of powerful forces, the immediate presence of terror and fear, a recognition and acceptance of the brutality of the natural world as well as the eternal insecurity of life. That these feelings are being experienced by many people throughout the world today is an unfortunate fact. . . . That is why we insist on subject matter, a subject matter that embraces these feelings and permits them to be expressed.[22]

There is no question that they were expressed. As Chave wrote apropos Rothko's turn to mythic material, and of his awareness of the world situation, his use of Greek tragedy was

> symptomatic of the desperation of these artists, who were searching urgently for a way to make a viable pictorial statement in the absence of an accepted rhetorical mode for doing so. Because circumstances of such epic proportions seem to demand an epic art, an effort was mounted to resuscitate what is for Western culture the paragon of epic art [Greek tragedy].[23]

I would add that the desperation these artists felt must in great measure have been derived from the fact that they were Jewish—a fact that does not directly appear in their work.

Of this group of artists, Newman, a reader of and about Jewish mystical texts, who gave biblical names to several paintings—*Abraham* (1949), *Covenant* (1949), and *Joshua* (1950)—identified most openly with Judaism. Acknowledging one's Jewish heritage, however, is not quite the same thing as creating works that directly reflect the Holocaust. Nonetheless, I believe that a strong argument can be made that the works for which Newman is justly famous, the stripe paintings—one or more vertical stripes on an uninflected field of color—were in part a response to the Holocaust as well as to the founding of the State of Israel. That is, among the abstract expressionists Newman was the most open and most responsive to the events and the aftermath of the war.

The immediate source for these paintings lay in Newman's reading of Gershom Scholem's account of Rabbi Isaac Luria, the sixteenth-century cabalist from Safad (now a town in Israel). Rabbi Luria explained that the world was created when God contracted into himself in order to create the primordial space for the world. Then God sent out a ray of light that set "the cosmic process in motion." Newman's single stripe down the length of a canvas represented that first ray of light, as well as the first human form. It was the moment of creation. Newman's biographer and friend, Thomas Hess, described Newman's thinking:

> The artist, Newman pointed out, must start like God, with chaos, the void. . . . Newman's first move is an act of division, straight down, creating an image. The image . . . reenacts God's primal gesture. . . . He [Newman] has taken his image of Genesis, of the creative act, of the artist as God.[24]

Since both Newman and Hess were Jewish, they must have known that Jews might want to act godlike and lead holy lives, but that Jews did not confuse themselves with (or find mystical union with) God. What might have prompted Newman to act with such radical individualism, to try to surmount, as it were, human limitations? He had written in 1948, in exaltation of the self, that "instead of making cathedrals out of Christ, man, or 'life,' we are making [them] out of ourselves, out of our feelings."[25] This was an extraordinary assertion of self-willed strength that had no precedent in the history of American art. It exalted the artist as a creator of something out of nothing, one whose creative powers rivaled that of the deity. One can read these lines as a paradigmatic Emersonian assertion of the power of the self or as an existential outburst of self-definition.

But Newman's statement and the stripe paintings—begun in 1948—should also be read as responses to the Holocaust as well as to the founding of the State of Israel, which occurred in the same year. No Jew could have remained unmoved by or neutral to either event. Newman's stripes, then, can be understood as an act of resistance to Jewish genocide and as a celebration of the birth and renewal of the Jewish state during a period of Jewish trauma and national revival. The stripes become his personal and solitary gesture, a raw assertion of self against a society and a God that perhaps did not merit his full respect. Newman's desire to make "cathedrals . . . out of ourselves" is both a reproach and a universalizing gesture that reaches out beyond Jewish identity to all humanity. It is an affirmation of individual strength and spirit in a world he wanted metaphorically to re-create. At the same time, although their acknowledged roots lie in Jewish mysticism, these works escape their parochiality, making an ideal parallel, it would seem, to the positions of Greenberg and Rosenberg.

No other artist, at that time or even in the succeeding decades, made such a heroic gesture. In Newman's work there is no sense of the victimization or brutality one finds in most Holocaust art, or of the sense of oppressive entrapment produced by all of those images of death, destruction and bestial behavior.

A group of paintings by Morris Louis (1912–1962), a second-generation abstract expressionist and color-field painter, is more typical of the work of both abstract and representational artists. In 1951 he made at least seven paintings that call to mind burnt sheets of paper or burnt books. Called the *Charred Journal* paintings, each consists of swirling, light-colored, jagged lines, suggesting exploded Hebrew letters, coursing over blackened grounds. Mira Goldfarb Berkowitz, in her study of these works, has provided a Holocaust context for understanding Louis's intentions. The Talmud states that even though Moses broke the first set of tablets containing the Ten Commandments, the letters, given by God, are immortal and imperishable, and therefore flew away to reassemble on another occasion. Linking these letters with those in the *Charred Journal* series, Berkowitz suggests that just as the letters of the Ten Commandments are indestructible, "so too are the letters of the burning books [Jewish scripture]. Louis has made a pictorial metaphor out of the scriptural one: that this culture, indeed its spirit, will survive. It will resist forces that seek to destroy it."[26]

Artists other than those associated with the New York avant-garde also responded to the Holocaust in the years during and after the war. Perhaps they responded even more profoundly and more often than did their literary counterparts. The responses, however, were rarely direct, in that biblical and mythological images were the primary vehicles for conveying the artists' feelings. Or the images might be so generalized that, to know the nature of the subject, one needs to read the title of a particular work or infer it from the artists' statements. At the same time one has to be wary of reading Holocaust presences into works that are innocent of them, unless one wants to argue—which I do not—that the subject was so overwhelming that it was inescapable, whether artists knew it or not.

Jacques Lipchitz (1891–1973) and Marc Chagall (1887–1985) were among the European artists who settled in New York City during the war. Just before and after he arrived in 1941, Lipchitz gave his works such titles as *Flight* (1940), *The Exile's Path* (1941), *The Rape of Europa* (1941), and *Theseus and the Minotaur* (1942). Chagall, after his arrival in 1941, also continued to explore imagery he had developed earlier, including that of the Wandering Jew and the crucified Jesus as well as the inhabitants of East European shtetls or villages. And Abraham Rattner (1895–1978), who returned to the United States in 1940 after living as an expatriate abroad, "kept his Jewish identity as low-keyed as possible, symbolizing the Holocaust and the war through his Crucifixions" during the early and middle 1940s. Only after 1947 did he begin to use biblical imagery as a way to confront the Holocaust.[27]

Hyman Bloom (born in 1913), an expressionist, resisted painting Holocaust scenes, explaining that the photographs of concentration camp corpses were too shocking for him. His Jewish consciousness would not let him distance himself far enough from them to allow him their use. But generalized images of death and decay did turn up in his postwar work, which combined private concerns with his reactions to the war. He said that his knowledge of prewar persecutions, which had been speculative, "gradually became a realized nightmare" during the war and were now "given [a] hideously present reality in Buchenwald and Auschwitz." To create these works he visited dissecting rooms in hospitals. Of Bloom's paintings of corpselike figures, art historian Sidney J. Freedberg noted an "affirmation of a perverse coloristic beauty," suggestive of "a continuity of some kind after death. In his paintings, the luminescent markings of decay upon the corpses are symptoms of the continuation of organic processes, the very activity of putrescence is a kind of victory over death."[28]

Comments like Freedberg's bespeak a mind still unable in 1949 to deal with the Holocaust, or one that still refused to connect what goes on in a painting by Bloom with rotting corpses in concentration camps, where death was death and not a victory of any sort. It should be viewed in its proper historical perspective, according to which many people, still clearly in some kind of denial, could neither understand nor find language to describe what had taken place in Europe.

Jack Levine, another expressionist who had used and would continue to use Jewish themes, bluntly stated that "the gas ovens were too horrible for me to face." Nor did he think of considering, like Chagall, the image of Jesus as a stand-in for persecuted modern Jewry. "Christ on the Cross is to me a symbol of Jewish persecution and nothing more, and I refuse to celebrate it," he said. And Baskin, too, could not deal directly with the Holocaust. Over the years he has responded by creating a race of damaged nude men instead.[29] Raphael Soyer (1899–1987) simply avoided the issue, finding it impossible to make paintings about the Holocaust as well as the atomic bombing of Japan and, later, the war in Vietnam because, as he said, "other media perform this function" better than the medium of painting.[30]

Soyer's response was not typical of the artists who had been associated with the Left during the 1930s. Several did make reference to the
Holocaust in their work, and among them, one of the angriest and
most engaged attitudes was revealed by William Gropper (1897–1977).

Gropper, who had pilloried the Jewish business and religious
establishments mercilessly during the 1930s, began to portray Nazi
brutality at least by 1943 when his book, *Your Brother's Blood Cries Out*,
was published. It contained eight lithographs, of which seven showed
imaginary re-creations of German activities. The eighth was of a group
of partisans, crouched behind a small mound, with only a few grenades
and rifles as well as a decrepit cannon, waiting for an attack. One of the
others shows, standing under a gallows, a group of laughing German
soldiers, one of whom is taking a picture of the four bodies hanging from
the crossbar. Still others show Germans herding people onto a train; carrying stolen booty, including a menorah, as they leave a pile of burning
bodies; and machine-gunning Jews.[31]

After a visit to Poland to witness the unveiling of a monument to
the Warsaw Ghetto in 1947, Gropper decided to make a series of paintings of individual rabbis, their arms raised, seemingly arguing with God.
Despite creating these works, he still felt that he had to qualify his
sense of Jewishness. Of them he said:

> I'm not Jewish in a professional sense, but in a human sense;
> here are six million destroyed. There is a ritual in the Jewish
> religion of lighting a candle for the dead, but instead of doing
> this, I decided to paint a picture in memory, every year. In this
> way, I paid my tribute, rather than burning a candle.

To make his point all the clearer, and perhaps also out of a need
to honor the left-wing concern for universalizing rather than particu-
larizing the horror of persecution, he said that he reacted to prejudice
and would react as any mistreated minority "because I have felt the same
things as a Jew, or my family has."[32]

Shahn seems to have had a more difficult time dealing with the
Holocaust in the immediate postwar years, and, I think, with his own
Jewishness as well. His aforementioned desire to avoid "ethnic self-pity,"
possibly a carryover from the days of the Communist Party's "third
period," might have been a factor. But since he included in his works
references to other ethnic groups, his ambivalence might have stemmed

in part from the very fact of his own Jewishness. Yet he did create works with Jewish content and often included Hebrew words in them. The degree to which he revealed his feelings can be inferred from the following passage from his book *The Shape of Content.* Some works, he said,

> had become more private and more inward-looking. A symbolism which I might have once considered cryptic now became the only means by which I could formulate the sense of emptiness and waste that the war gave me, and the sense of the littleness of people trying to live on through the enormity of war. I was very little concerned with communication as a conscious objective. Formulation itself was enough of a problem—to formulate into images, into painted surfaces, feelings, which if obscure, were at least strongly felt.[33]

Clearly, if Shahn had the Holocaust in mind, he had subsumed it within his reactions to the war in general. But as Ziva Amishai-Maisels has pointed out, Shahn, like other artists, reidentified with Judaism after the full extent of the Holocaust became known. But when he did create a work with Holocaust overtones, he used a symbolic, even private language that would be known primarily to those who could read Hebrew, a kind of closet text. For example, in his *Sound in the Mulberry Trees* (1948), a boy sits on a tenement stoop blowing bubble gum and a girl looks at a store window. There is a scroll in the window with a Hebrew inscription from 2 Sam. 5:24, which reads:

> And let it be, when thou hearest the sound of a going in the tops of the mulberry trees, that thou shalt bestir thyself; for then shall the Lord go out before thee, to smite the host of the Philistines.

Since this verse concerns David's approaching victory over the Philistines, and since the painting was created in 1948, the year of the founding of the State of Israel, Shahn may perhaps have been referring to the War of Independence.[34] Compared to, say, Newman's stripe paintings, the Jewish references are more overt because of the Hebrew lettering, but the Holocaust references are equally covert as well as emotionally contained, unless one is quite familiar with the Bible. There is none of Newman's implied exaltation over the founding of the modern State of Israel.

Shahn's Holocaust references tended to be biblical rather than contemporary. For example, he included the following lines from Jer. 9:1 in *And Mine Eyes a Fountain of Tears* (1965), a serigraph of a woman's head:

Oh that my head were waters, and mine eyes a fountain of tears, that I might weep day and night for the slain of the daughter of my people!

The artist Ben-Zion was much more comfortable with his Jewish identity. Born in Ukraine in 1897, he immigrated to the United States in 1920 and became part of the Jewish artistic and literary world in New York City soon after his arrival. The son of a cantor steeped in Jewish culture and religion, he, too, during the 1940s turned to Holocaust imagery, which, like Shahn's and Rattner's, tended to invoke biblical and patriarchal figures. But he was one of the very few Jewish artists who used this subject matter without apology or seeming embarrassment. In fact, during the 1940s and 1950s, he explored biblical imagery (without Holocaust resonances) to a greater extent than anybody else, and clearly delighted in doing so. As he wrote in the 1960s:

Although identification of an artist must be first and foremost with humanity as a whole, nevertheless the really genuine one never dissociates himself from his creed. On the contrary, he thrives on the sources of his origin, and through his background reaches humanity which no matter how multiple and different its creeds and upbringing may be—at the roots is the same humanity. The true artist, then, while remaining in touch with his background rises above provincial, nationalistic, or religious bigotry.[35]

This is very much an example of the kind of thinking that holds that through the local one can find the universal, and that the universal can be found through the local. Ben-Zion, then, found his source of inspiration, recognizably so, in his particular background, though he did not necessarily want to be limited by it.

He turned to the Holocaust as a theme before the end of the war. His major work on that event, the series *De Profundis*, composed of ten gouaches and two oils, was exhibited in 1946 (fig. 3). In his catalog statement, he explained why he chose certain subjects:

As people and countries are counting their losses after the defeat of the destroyers of Europe, the tribute of six million Jewish people, extinguished in the most fiendish way, has scarcely penetrated our conscience, and we are still far from being able to create an adequate symbol for this plight. As one who identifies with the massacred ones, and as an artist, I could not restrain personal expression of grief. If the patri-archic types of Jews have dominated my conceptions, it is because they were the backbone of the nation and its cultural source. It is their children and grandchildren, migrating to western Europe and America, who contributed so much to the culture and civilization of their adopted countries. I chose them also because their humiliation was the deepest, for they had the strength of character and rare courage to keep their belief and mode of life inwardly as well as outwardly—and because the mockery of the murderers must have reached hell's hilarity in handling these martyrs.[36]

Finding his subject matter in patriarchal figures, Ben-Zion, like Shahn and Rattner, fell back on stereotypical and communal figures. Evidently this has been a Jewish tradition in art, literature, and life, for, as historian David Roskies has pointed out, "the greater the catastrophe, the more the Jews have recalled the ancient prototypes. . . . This sense of recapitulation is a constant in Jewish history."[37] As a result the particular cataclysm, in this instance the Holocaust, is located on a continuum of Jewish experience and is therefore incorporated into Jewish memory and Jewish history. The assumption is that communal memory continues. Ideally the response to the cataclysm could have a unifying effect if the majority understood the codes and traditions. (In this view the Holocaust is a variant on the destruction of Solomon's Temple in Jerusalem. Recent events could be read in light of an image of that destruction.)

The philosopher Emil Fackenheim explained the use of this tradition in the following way. He posited the idea that there were non-Jewish Jewish thinkers and Jewish-Jewish thinkers. The non-Jewish Jewish thinkers, which included leftists, might still see a future bright with some sort of humanitarian promise. Fackenheim thought this was essentially an escapist position, an escape into a future that probably would not happen. By contrast, Jewish-Jewish thinkers escaped into the past, the Jewish past filled with wisdom, faith, and succor. From the vantage point of this past, the Holocaust could be seen as just one more chapter in Jewish history, albeit a monstrously horrendous one.[38]

In this view the Holocaust is rooted in postbiblical rabbinic literature, according to which contemporary events were subsumed within biblical tradition and biblical interpretations of events (for example, pogroms during the Crusades were considered in relation to the destruction of the Temple in Jerusalem).[39] I do not know the degree to which Ben-Zion's religiosity, as well as the remembered childhood training in Bible studies of other artists such as Shahn and Rattner, might have prompted them to highlight this kind of reading of contemporary events, but the tradition was clearly still strong among them.

Ben-Zion certainly, and the others to a reasonable extent, could be called Jewish-Jewish artists. And it is true that their art does allow for community grief through direct or indirect allusions to, say, the Book of Job or to Lamentations. But some problems immediately arise. Since Ben-Zion said in the aforementioned catalog statement: "We are still far from being able to create an adequate symbol for this plight," I would like to pursue this line of inquiry a bit further, to locate it within one kind of Jewish perspective.

Their work, evocative as it may be, simplifies current history and becomes part of a monolithic communal Jewish memory to which many modern Jews (in the 1940s and certainly after) have little or no connection. Further, images of people with sad faces or wringing their hands or wearing biblical garb do not allow an immediate personal response on the part of the viewer. If anything, substituting biblical for contemporary memory becomes a form of antimemory, in that it places parameters around a true picture of the suffering induced by the Holocaust and the kinds of responses available to the modern observer.[40] Furthermore, I am not the first person to believe that the Holocaust was unique in history, and from this point of view two questions emerge— can old-fashioned responses and the use of archetypal or biblical figures remain credible for any length of time to a Jewish experience different in kind from earlier ones, and can these figures communicate much to succeeding generations that no longer participate in collective memories based on shared faith and customs?

Yet another issue needs to be raised. Ben-Zion and many others over the succeeding decades have referred to the victims as martyrs.

Artists have used images of Jesus and Job-like figures to invoke the brutality of the Holocaust. However, presenting these and other biblical figures implies that there is a purpose, a redeeming meaning to death. Martyrs die out of choice and/or a sense of duty. The Jewish rabbis and teachers murdered by the Romans, for example, chose death rather than give up their religion. By contrast, the deaths of those murdered in the Holocaust were only about murder. It really is impossible to believe that the murder of six million Jewish people was part of a divine plan or vision. Lawrence Langer summed up this point of view succinctly when he wrote that the Holocaust "was not part of a divine plan, but a human one."[41] There were no choices to be made in Hitler's Europe, no religious conversions, no decisions to accept Nazi race laws. There was just murder.

Biblical and patriarchal imagery, then, while comforting, may not be entirely relevant and may even render visually the Holocaust more harmless than it was. As Fackenheim has said,

> The Holocaust did not present itself as demanding the response of martyrdom. . . . The Nazi empire, far from repeating the Roman folly of creating Jewish martyrs, was on the contrary cunningly designed to murder Jewish martyrdom. . . . Within the Nazi universe, what mattered was only that Jews existed; as for their beliefs or their deeds, and indeed especially, when they were saintly or heroic, they were of no account. As for us who come after, of all things unbearable about the Holocaust, the most unbearable, and most necessary to remember and therefore to bear, are not the prayers of the martyrs or the hero's death of the fighters, but rather the cry of innocence that comes to us from all those who *did not, or could not, or would not choose* [italics in original] heroism or martyrdom or any of the ways in which men and women throughout the ages have managed to give meaning to death.[42]

From this point of view, disputed by those who believe that—however inconceivable it might be—the Holocaust was part of God's plan, one mourns the dead as murdered individuals, not as stereotypical martyrs.

There is still another point to ponder, however. Artists, writers, and filmmakers did not create their works for scholars to evaluate in their studies, but as ways to express feelings about the Holocaust and perhaps to help exorcise its impact on them. Whether this means reaching into the biblical or mythological past; confronting the 1940s books and newspaper headlines about and photographs of the camps; or fantasizing an ideal future is an entirely individual decision. Making art about the Holocaust is a personal way of witnessing, of commemorating, and questions about how one should or should not proceed are really irrelevant. There is no "proper" point of entry into any sort of narrative about the Holocaust, no appropriate way to establish a bond between the dead and the living or between the past and the present. "The insoluble riddle of the Holocaust," as Langer has pointed out, "[is] how to establish a connection between consequential living and inconsequential dying."[43]

Postwar Responses

Changes in Attitude

Several observers and commentators have noticed that in the postwar years a "willed amnesia and [a] self-imposed silence" characterized the Jewish-American community's response to the Holocaust.[1] Many Jewish Americans wanted to acculturate and, beyond that, even assimilate into American life rather than retain a particularist Jewish identity. Vast numbers moved to the suburbs and either dropped out of Jewish life or developed communal ties quite different from those that bound ghetto residents to one another. American values of autonomy and personal fulfillment replaced older notions of community involvement and Jewish identity formation. It has been even suggested that "to some extent, the breakdown in community has negatively affected the availability of sophisticated audiences for Jewish poets, dramatists, and others in artistic endeavors." In the words of one observer: "As the story of Lot's wife illustrates, a person cannot afford to look back while fleeing."[2]

Few wanted to identify with the helpless victims of the war or with survivors, who perhaps could not communicate easily with others and often seemed to be defeated persons. Since many of them felt guilty over the very fact of having survived, and for not having responded more militantly, they were inhibited about revealing their horrendous experiences.

In many instances survivors have learned to remain silent when, after being asked about their experiences, their answers are ignored by people who do not really want to hear them. Furthermore, soon after the end of the war, the former Federal Republic of Germany became an ally, so the general mood was to let bygones be bygones.

In the mid-1950s, however, postwar numbness began to give way. The publication in 1953 of the English translation of *Anne Frank: The Diary of a Young Girl* (adapted for the stage in 1955 and the screen in 1959) and in 1960 of *Night,* Elie Wiesel's Holocaust memoir, bespoke new interest in, and response to, Holocaust-related issues. In 1960 the Eichmann trial in Jerusalem generated great interest, and Raul Hilberg's *The Destruction of the European Jews* appeared the following year. The Arab-Israeli wars of 1967 and 1973 generated a tremendous outpouring of sentiment for Israel. Its success in those wars provided Jewish Americans with a Jewish self-confidence they had not previously possessed, and also enabled them to identify as Jewish in a cultural and social rather than in a religious way. Being Jewish was no longer circumscribed by bigotry, murder, and humiliation, but by positive experiences. At the same time, as historian Edward S. Shapiro has pointed out, "Memories of the Holocaust strengthened the ardor of American Jews for Israel, while the perilous situation of Israel in the 1960s encouraged Jews to bring into the open the hurt they carried because of the Holocaust." And as author Judith Miller has suggested, since "Jews no longer felt so absolutely vulnerable, they could finally confront the period of their most intense vulnerability."[3]

As the decades wear on, facing the savagery of the Holocaust directly has become common. For Jews, acknowledging its grip on one's thoughts has become almost a natural reflex. I have heard young people born years after the end of the war say that the Holocaust is the central event of their lives. And writers have been sharing in print feelings that would have been impossible to contemplate so openly in the 1940s and early 1950s. Langer, for example, felt that "the ordeal of European Jewry is over for the victims; [but] it will never be over for us." Levi said much the same thing: "It must be observed mournfully, that the injury cannot be healed: it extends through time." George Steiner agreed when he wrote: "The idea that Jews everywhere have been maimed by the European catastrophe, that the massacre has left all who survived (even if they were nowhere near the actual scene) off balance, as does the tearing of a limb, is one which American Jews can understand in an intellectual sense."

In the years since 1966, when Steiner's comments were published, American Jews have reacted in a much more emotional and visceral way, as well as an intellectual one. Author Leonard Fein has observed that "to be a Jew in America is to carry with you the consciousness of limitless savagery. It is to carry that consciousness with you not as an abstraction, but as a reality; not, God help us all, only as a memory, but also as a possibility." An even more empathic response to the Holocaust was expressed by art critic Donald Kuspit when discussing the works of Natan Nuchi (fig. 31): "Every Jew has a Holocaust within him; in his most innermost heart he has gone up in smoke or been starved to death after being castrated by society." Probably all these figures would understand literary critic Alfred Kazin (whose own thoughts about his Jewishness had evidently changed since the 1940s and 1950s) when he wrote in the 1970s that the Holocaust is the "nightmare . . . that will haunt me to my last breath."[4]

Open and continuous acknowledgment of the horrors of the Holocaust gained in importance as age also began to take its toll of survivors. The realization that their stories needed to be told and that people needed to remember became compelling reasons to learn as much as possible as soon as possible. Furthermore, in the world of Jewish organizations as well as in the minds of many individuals, a feeling began to grow that the Holocaust was being subsumed within other holocausts, and that it was important to keep it Judaized. Beyond that, the deniers had to be answered, a task that grew even more urgent when one so prominent as Patrick Buchanan, a serious presidential candidate in 1992 and 1996, "proclaimed his skepticism about whether hundreds of thousands of Jews had been executed at Treblinka."[5]

Encouraged by the various liberation movements of the 1960s and 1970s—black, feminist, gay—Jews found value in identifying openly and publicly as Jewish. But questions remained as to how this was to be accomplished. Most identifying signs, such as synagogue attendance or speaking Yiddish, were no longer common. Lighting Sabbath candles was for one's grandparents or for the religious. The cabalah was for the studious and the spiritual. But acknowledgment and commemoration of the Holocaust were for everybody, and thus became one of the most visible signs of Jewish identity: It could be used at will and when needed.

Ironically its popularity as a means of identity—as a substitute for actually developing a Jewish life, whatever that might mean—has been called into question. For example, one observer asserted that "the fires of Hell are mesmerizing, but Jews cannot organize their future solely by that light." Another held that "the continuity of Jewish identity must be grounded in some form of distinctive everyday practice," and still others have suggested that "remembrance of the tragedy cannot serve as a stand-in for a live ethnic culture."[6]

As valid as such statements may be, the fact remains that the Holocaust is a major galvanizing force in the Jewish-American community. As author Anne Roiphe has written: "For many of us the Holocaust marks the end of religion, but paradoxically enough [it] simultaneously marks the point of reconnection of [the] assimilated Jew to Jewishness, to tradition, to history, to bloodlines." Interest in it has helped to reestablish Jewish memory cut short by the Holocaust itself and by assimilation into American life. For writers and artists the use of Holocaust materials and imagery has become a kind of spiritual resistance to a world still perceived as antagonistic to Judaism. These materials and images also provide writers and artists with a moral purpose in a time of postmodernism. Such imagery can also help people understand the suffering of others: It brings them closer to the central Jewish experience of the twentieth century and provides a way to "move . . . into the pain and hence the meaning of the Holocaust," which might in itself be considered a kind of memorial. And, finally, the use of Holocaust imagery, in the decades when actual memories are growing dim enough that their ultimate disappearance may be in sight, allows artists and viewers not just the ability to bear witness "but rather to keep [the events] before our eyes. Testimony is to be a means of transmission to future generations."[7]

Harold Paris and Leon Golub

In the years immediately after the war, younger American artists tended to avoid the Holocaust as subject matter, or at least it is difficult to find such imagery suggested in their work. Two did respond, however. Both had been in the army, and both had been stationed in

Europe. One, Harold Paris, saw the camp at Buchenwald; the other, Leon Golub, saw photographs of the camps. Both obviously witnessed the devastating effects of the war on local populations, their homes, and their cities. In some measure they never quite recovered from or forgot their firsthand experiences.

Paris's work is more traditional in that—by comparison to Golub's more assertive and violent forms—he created images of passive victims and devouring creatures, and he also made environments that act as memorials to the victims. In 1948 and 1949, in response to what he had seen at Buchenwald in 1945 (when he was barely twenty), he made a series of nine prints entitled *Buchenwald* (fig. 4). Very stylized and highly expressive, the figures take stock poses. Similar to Ben-Zion, who also used traditional subject matter, Paris fell back on stereotypical images.

But Paris's rage grew, and both his subject matter and his imagery changed. By 1953 he had created a series of prints based on the theme of Moloch, the ancient figure who ate his own children. These works are characterized by thickened and intentionally messy and sketchlike black lines—which, in at least one instance—show a small child being consumed by a monstrous-looking Moloch. Of these prints Paris said that he was "concerned with the forces of good and evil that exist not only in man but in myself." Given the grotesque qualities of these images, Paris was evidently more concerned with the forces of evil in man than with anything else.[8]

Thinking and reading about the Holocaust over a period of years means always coming upon something worse—something even more inconceivable—that people experienced and lived to tell about. And then you read further, and so on. Or a survivor will tell you something in your wildest imagination you could not imagine anybody doing to another human being. The more you find out, the less you understand. There is no bottom or end to it; you are caught between numbness and rage. Paris must have felt both when in 1969 he began to make his *Kaddish* environments. These culminated in his *Koddesh-Koddashim* (1972), a sealed room based on the small space called the Holy of Holies in the Temple in Jerusalem, which only the high priest could enter once a year on Yom Kippur, the holiest day of the Jewish year. Paris added the prayer for the dead, the *Kaddish*. He asked, "What does it look like?" and answered, "Like the inside of my soul." And he asked again, "What is inside?" and answered, "All my dreams of the outside."[9] In short, so overwhelming were the effects of what he had read and seen that he could not find the visual (or verbal) language to articulate his feelings. They were all literally and figuratively bottled up in that sealed room.

A few years later, in 1975, Paris created an environment for the Jewish Museum in New York City entitled *Kaddish for the Little Children,* based in part on the poetry and drawings of children held in Terezín. In a dimly lit room, black sand covered a black brick floor to evoke "the thought of children's tears of blood." Three brick staircases led nowhere. The dominant mood was one of transience and loss.[10]

These environments date from the 1970s. In comparison with earlier works by Paris and by artists of the previous generation, they reveal a more direct response, a characteristic of more recent works on Holocaust themes. Their subject matter is not deflected through biblical or mythological themes. Nor is the content universalized to soften and diffuse the impact of the Holocaust.

Leon Golub's works of the late 1940s and 1950s, however, were probably the first responses by a Jewish-American artist in which the reaction of rage was both unmediated and openly expressed. For many years nobody followed his lead. Thus his early works are unique in the history of this type of imagery in the United States. They begin as early as 1946 with works such as *Charnel House* (fig. 5) and *Evisceration* and continue through the *Burnt Man* series of the early 1950s. To be sure, these works also convey Golub's feelings about individual identity, power, and sanctity in modern society, but the Holocaust resonances are undeniable. Of these works Golub has said, "I think the first paintings I was doing when I started school [the school of the Art Institute of Chicago in 1946] were concentration-camp scenes." Composed of figures vaporizing in flames, eviscerated and flayed, Golub wanted to make images about world horrors in as blunt a way as possible.[11]

Meaning in these works oscillates between Golub's understanding of himself as a Jew and as an individual in late-twentieth-century Western culture. As he has explained: "I'm a Jew. Many of my friends were Jews. It was a shocking incredible thing [the Holocaust]. But that's not all of it. It also had to do with this sense I had of myself as *estranged—* as marginalized." Recognition of his estrangement, of what he called "domination and violence, of existential fatality," was based not solely on his Jewishness, although, as he has indicated to me, he certainly did not like the idea that as a Jew he was automatically a victim, but also on his understanding of relationships between governments and individuals as well as between individuals in the postwar world.

So, on the one hand, as Kuspit suggests, in their revelation of the savagery visited on its victims, Golub's works are his Jewish revenge on Western civilization. "Through Golub's work, our time will live in memory as monstrous and rotten." Of the figure painted in *Thwarted* (1953), a frontally placed large torso, flayed, based on the idealized classical Belvedere Torso in the Vatican Museum, Kuspit sees a concentration-camp figure "haunting the world, a dead creature distorted with the lust for revenge." On the other hand, Golub himself discerns a universal element in these figures. On one occasion he said: "Man is seen as having undergone a holocaust or facing annihilation or mutation. The ambiguities of these huge forms indicate the stress of their vulnerability versus their capacities for endurance." On another occasion, discussing figures he had made in the 1970s, he commented that he was

> concerned with the burnt experiences of the twentieth century. I combine concerns of how man operates in the world and what happens when he loses control. I go to sources which give me information . . . on experience becoming catastrophic. . . . The question is who am I painting? . . . I am painting these warrior-citizens in the most extreme of human conditions, the response to terror. Dachau, Hiroshima, Vietnam.[12]

With the mention of Hiroshima and Vietnam, a point needs to be made. It has often been said that during World War II, Jews were not the only ones who suffered. Many Slavs, Gypsies, and homosexuals were also singled out for annihilation. Genocide has also been seen in Armenia, Cambodia, Rwanda, and the former Yugoslavia. But many people insist that the Holocaust was, unfortunately, special, and that it was different in kind from other genocides. Nevertheless it was the fear of folding the Holocaust into other events of extreme brutality in modern human history, of diffusing its specialness, that prompted literary critic Alvin Rosenfeld to respond: "To generalize or universalize the victims of the Holocaust is not only to profane their memories but to exonerate their executioners." Or, as film historian Ilan Avisar asserted even more strongly: "The refusal to acknowledge that the perpetrators of the incomparable crime were Germans and that the main victims were Jews means ignoring crucial facts of history, thereby blocking any avenues toward the possibility of comprehending this monstrous tragedy."[13] Although the great majority of artists acknowledge the uniqueness of the Jewish genocide during World War II, at the same time, invoking their Jewish heritage of social justice when discussing their Holocaust works, they have voiced their opposition to oppression at other times in history. That is, they have not and do not intend to diminish the Holocaust but have acknowledged other holocausts that occurred elsewhere in the world. Golub and others do not deny the centrality of the Holocaust as a motivating agent in their work.

Pride in Their Heritage

Since the 1960s many Jewish-American artists have chosen to remember the Holocaust and to make it, in many instances, a central element of their work. Together with other artists who find inspiration in the Bible, the cabalah, and other aspects of Jewish life, they have created an explosion of Jewish art, or rather an explosion of Jewish subject matter in art, in the last few decades. These artists, like, say, klezmer musicians, rejoice, even, exult in, their Jewish heritage. Even those who reject the religious aspects of Judaism still find in its culture a vast resource to explore, an intriguing repository of their heritage as well as a justification for social commitment through art. This last point is of some interest because, whereas the generation of the 1930s justified social commitment through political action, the present one finds it within Judaism. That is, contemporary artists do not run from Judaism as earlier artists did, but find in it and through it a way to remain Jewish, American, and socially active at the same time. Comfortable in their Americanness, they can acknowledge their Jewishness.

Several, whether they use Holocaust imagery or not, are proud to declare publicly their Jewishness in ways that previous generations simply could not. For example, Vera Klement, born in Danzig in 1929, has said that "being a Jew, a woman, a survivor, are at the center of how I describe the world." Louise Fishman (born in 1939) has stated: "The influence of Judaism on my work is profound." Several artists from California, where there are strong centers of Jewish art activity in Los Angeles and the San Francisco Bay area, have written about their identity as artists and as Jews. Harry Clewans has said: "I am a Jew. To put it simply, this is what motivates me to paint as I do." Mary Bikszer believes it to be impossible to "separate my art from my Jewish [American] and Israeli identity. . . . I am proud of my past, my deep roots, which

Fig. 1. Diego Rivera, "Hitler" panel, from *America Today.*

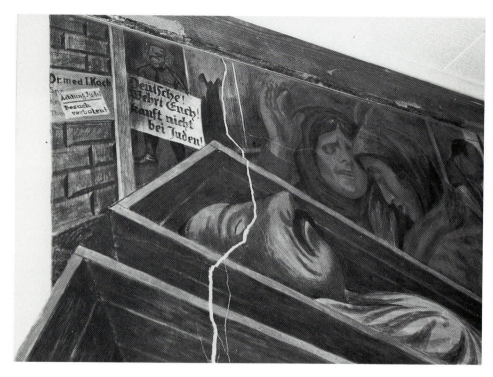

Fig. 2. Ben Shahn, mural in Community Center, Roosevelt, New Jersey, 1937–1938 (detail).

Fig. 3. Ben-Zion, *De Profundis: In Memory of the Massacred Jews of Nazi Europe,* 1943, gouache and ink, 24" × 19". *(Museum of Modern Art, New York, given anonymously; photo © 1996 Museum of Modern Art, New York)*

Fig. 4. Harold Paris, "Where Are We Going?" plate 2 from *Buchenwald* series of nine plates, 1948, engraving on lucite, printed in black, 12 1/4" × 23 3/4". *(Museum of Modern Art, New York purchase; photo © 1992 Museum of Modern Art, New York)*

Fig. 5. Leon Golub, *Charnel House*, 1946, lithograph, 15" × 19". *(Courtesy Leon Golub)*

Fig. 6. Tibor R. Spitz,
March to Eternity, 1983,
oil, 31" × 31".
(Courtesy Tibor R. Spitz)

Fig. 7. Sidney Chafetz, *Rudolph Hess*, 1991, lithograph, 35" × 25". (*Courtesy Sidney Chafetz*)

Fig. 8. Eleanor Antin, *Vilna Nights*, 1993, mixed media installation. *(Courtesy Ronald Feldman Fine Arts, New York; photo, Jewish Museum/Art Resource, New York)*

Fig. 9. Murray Zimiles, "Untitled," from the *Book of Fire*, 1990–1991, lithograph, 38" × 50". *(Courtesy Murray Zimiles)*

Fig. 10. Judith Goldstein, *The Burning Barn*, 1995, acrylic/collage, 24" × 36". *(Courtesy Judith Goldstein)*

Fig. 11. Louise Kramer, *Kaunas, Lithuania: Women and Children Rounded Up, Told to Undress, The Marched to the Death Pits and Shot, 1990s*, clay, 9" × 15" × 26". *(Courtesy Louise Kramer)*

Fig. 12. Hannelore Baron, *Untitled*, 1984, assemblage, 7" × 5 1/2" × 2 1/2". *(Gallery Schlesinger, New York)*

Fig. 13. Kitty Klaidman,
Looking Down II,
1991, acrylic on paper,
40" × 60".
*(Colonel Jonathan
Berman Collection)*

Fig. 14. Philip Orenstein, *Fall of Paris, June 14, 1940*, 1993, mixed media on canvas, 84" × 288".
(Courtesy Philip Orenstein)

Fig. 15. Elyse Klaidman, *The Tracks,* 1993, oil on canvas, 28" × 22". *(Courtesy Elyse Klaidman)*

Fig. 16. Debbie Teicholz, "Untitled," from *Prayer by the Wall,* 1991, photomontage, 35" × 64". *(Courtesy Debbie Teicholz)*

Fig. 17. Wendy Joy
Kupperman,
*The Far Country #1:
Auschwitz Icon,*
1992–1993,
photograph.
*(Courtesy Wendy Joy
Kuppermann)*

Fig. 18. Daisy Brand, *Epilogue,*
1994, porcelain, earthenware,
and wood, 26" × 18 1/2".
(Courtesy Daisy Brand)

Fig. 19. Alice Lok Cahana, *No Names*, ca. 1980, acrylic on canvas, 46" × 85".
(Courtesy Alice Lok Cahana)

Fig. 20. Gerda Meyer-Bernstein, *Block 11*, 1989, mixed media, 300" × 420".
(Courtesy Gerda Meyer-Bernstein)

Fig. 21. Anna Bialobroda, *Violation*, 1986, acrylic on canvas, 60" × 65".
(Courtesy Anna Bialobroda)

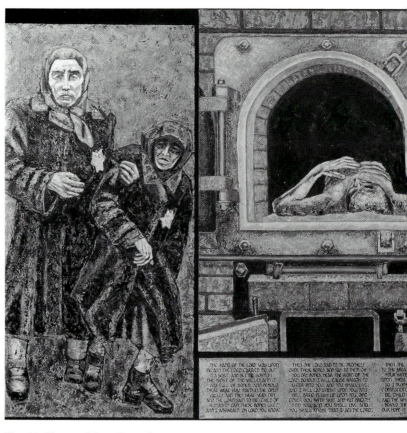

Fig. 22. Howard Lee Oransky,
Will These Bones Live?,
1990–1994, oil, gouache, and
ink on linen and canvas,
80" × 132".
(Courtesy Howard Lee Oransky)

Fig. 23. Mindy Weisel,
Who's the Driver?, 1984,
watercolor, 30" × 40".
(Courtesy Mindy Weisel)

Fig. 24. Marty Kalb, *They No
Longer Cry*, 1993, acrylic on
wood and tar paper, 80" × 144".
(Courtesy Marty J. Kalb)

Fig. 25. Aharon
Gluska, *Identity
Pending II,* 1993–1994,
mixed media on
canvas, 66" × 57".
*(Courtesy
Aharon Gluska)*

Fig. 26. Jerome Witkin, *The Butcher's Helper,*
Buchenwald, 1941–1945, 1991, 348" long
(panels 2 and 3). *(Courtesy Jerome Witkin)*

Fig. 27. Pearl Hirshfield,
Shadows of Auschwitz,
1989, mixed media
installation, 72" × 216".
(Courtesy Pearl Hirshfield)

Fig. 28. Arie A. Galles, *Chelmno,* from *Fourteen Stations Suite,* 1995, charcoal and white conté crayon, 47 1/2" × 75". *(Photo, Tim Volk)*

Fig. 29. Ruth Wesiberg, from the "Redemption" section of *The Scroll,* 1987, drawing with color wash, 39" × 1,128". *(Hebrew Union College Skirball Museum, Los Angeles, gift of Sandy and Adrea Bettelman in memory of Al Bettelman)*

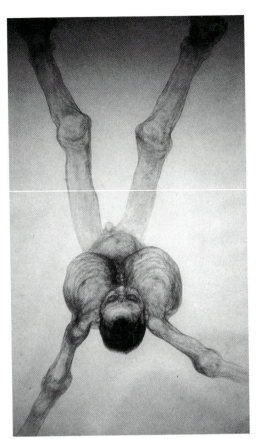

Fig. 30. Selma Waldman, "The Sticks" from *Falling Man*. 1966, charcoal, umber, ochre, and sienna chalks on paper. *(Courtesy Selma Waldman)*

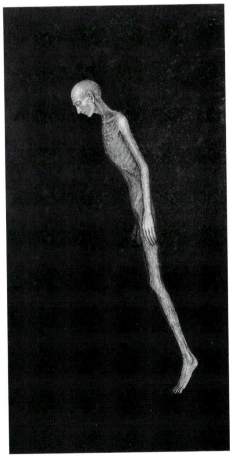

Fig. 31. Natan Nuchi, *Untitled*, 1990, acrylic on canvas, 88" × 44". *(Courtesy Natan Nuchi)*

Fig. 32. Audrey Flack, *World War II (Vanitas)*, incorporating a portion of the Margaret Bourke-White photograph *Buchenwald, April 1945*, copyright © Time Inc., 1976–1977, oil over acrylic on canvas, 96" × 96". *(Courtesy Louis K. Meisel Gallery, New York, photo, Bruce C. Jones)*

Fig. 33. Marlene E. Miller, *Schlafwagen: Who Will Say Kaddish For Them?*, 1993–1994, mixed media, 60" × 24" × 24". *(Courtesy Marlene E. Miller)*

Fig. 34. Tobi Kahn, "Brun," from *The Shrine Series*, 1985, acrylic on wood and bronze, 21" × 11" × 9 1/4". *(Courtesy, Tobi Kahn, photo, Adam Reich)*

Fig. 35. Grace Graupe-Pillard, *Nowhere to Go II*—"Family Tree," 1990, mixed media on cut-out canvas, 79 1/2" × 70". *(Courtesy Grace Graupe-Pillard)*

Fig. 36. Gabrielle Rossmer, *Garment*, 1994, stiffened cloth, 108" × 40" × 8". *(Courtesy Gabrielle Rossmer; photo, George Vasquez)*

Fig. 37. Ellen Rothenberg, *Partial Index,*
from *The Anne Frank Project,* 1990–1991,
mixed media installation, 480" × 144".
(Photo, Kent Gallery, New York)

Fig. 38. Nancy Spero,
Masha Bruskina, 1992,
handprinting and
printed collage on paper,
24 1/2" × 19 1/2".
*(Courtesy Nancy Spero;
photo, David Reynolds)*

Fig. 39. Joan Snyder, *Women in Camps*, 1988, oil and acrylic on linen mounted on board with photographic image, 22" × 48". *(Courtesy Hirschl & Adler Modern, New York; photo, Zindman/Fremont)*

the Moon
SHone
in
Germany
The Moon
SHines
in
Palestine
And
MEN ARE
STILL
SEEKING
FinAL
SoLuTions

DEATH CAMPS

Fig. 40. Jeffrey A. Wolin, *Rena Grynblat, Born 1926, Warsaw, Poland,* photograph. *(Courtesy Catherine Edelman Gallery, Chicago)*

Fig. 41. Pier Marton, entrance to *Jew,* 1990 video installation at Spertus Museum, Chicago. *(Courtesy Pier Marton; photo Pier Marton)*

Fig. 42. Susan Erony, *Memorial to the Jews of Lodz #4*, 1990, found Hebrew texts, acrylic, and lead on canvas. 14" × 11". *(Courtesy Susan Erony)*

Fig. 43. Ellen K. Levy, *Construction Site (Synagogue in Budapest)*, 1995, oil on wood, 12" × 16". *(Courtesy Associated American Artists, New York)*

Fig. 44. Edith Altman, *Reclaiming the Symbol/The Art of Memory*, 1988–1992, mixed media installation, varying dimensions. *(Courtesy Edith Altman)*

are rich in beautiful symbols, and profound ideas for all mankind and for my people." And Gertrude T. Bleiberg has "always felt strongly about my Jewish identity, and even through I don't always use Jewish themes, I consider all my work to be Jewish."[14]

The assertion of Jewish identity is in part an outgrowth of mainstream acceptance as well as the ability to feel comfortable as assimilated Americans. Strength can be gained from acknowledging one's Jewish as well as American heritage. Wendy Joy Kuppermann, who incorporates Holocaust imagery into her photographs, has searched for the proper formulation of her now proud joint heritage (fig. 17). A child of survivors, she has most recently stated: "At heart I am an American artist. At core I am an American dream risen curling like smoke from the ovens of Auschwitz. . . . At heart I am an American artist. At core I am an American Jew come home from the far reaches of sorrow."[15]

But that very acceptance of the United States as the new homeland has created some unease. It can lead to complete assimilation, which many artists resist. Painting Jewish themes or what some call "painting from a Jewish point of view," however defined, is a way to maintain a sense of Jewish identity. Yet some realize that acceptance can also lead to a false sense of security, as if all identity problems are resolved, and marginalization in the art world and in the public sphere no longer exist. Archi Rand, one of the most visible "Jewish" artists, has said: "I announce my Jewishness, knowing that there is a potentially hostile, if not lethal 'other' out there. The 'other's' existence and makeup may be a myth, but my instinct says no. In fear, I hold tight to what has nourished me in exile."[16]

With these words Rand articulates the thoughts of other artists with whom I have corresponded. They are American but also Jews, an acknowledgment in which resides some fear, which will probably never vanish, as well as a note of defiance. There is also recognition of a kind of spiritual sustenance as well as pride in Jewish culture and Jewish religion that cannot be found elsewhere.

These characteristics appear among artists who have used Holocaust imagery since the 1970s. In terms of the sheer numbers, it appears that many turned to such imagery in the 1980s, according to the correspondence I have had with them. For some artists, particularly survivors and children of survivors, trips to the family shtetl in Europe as well as to the sites of various concentration camps triggered an outpouring of work on Holocaust themes. For these artists such travel was emotionally and psychologically impossible before the 1980s. Afterward employing this imagery became part of a healing process that will no doubt continue for years to come. There seems to be no other overriding reason for the burgeoning use of Holocaust materials. Nor are there developmental sequences according to which styles or media applications have changed in some sort of logical progression over the decades.

One searches in vain, as well, for a single profile that fits the majority of artists, or a single rubric that encompasses them other than their commitment to using Holocaust materials. The artists include those who experienced Nazi terror during the 1930s but left Europe before the start of the war, survivors of the camps, children hidden during the war by gentiles, children of survivors, and those who had no direct contact with the Holocaust either because they were born after the war or because they were born in countries or places beyond the reach of the German military and its collaborators.

For some the creation of one work to commemorate or acknowledge the Holocaust seems to have been sufficient. For others the Holocaust is inscribed in virtually everything they have done. Styles range from the representational to the abstract. Some artists use traditional media, and others use collage, found objects, film, video, and photographs. Some create environments evocative of life in Europe either in or outside the camps during the 1940s, and others use documentary photographs of the camps as source material. Still others freely invent subject matter. Their attitudes range from a universalist one in which the Holocaust—although certainly acknowledged as a terrible and central event in Jewish history—is just another example of inhuman behavior, to a sharply focused one in which, as philosopher Vladimir Jankelevitch declares: "The extermination of the Jews was not . . . a sudden outbreak of violence; it was doctrinally founded, philosophically explained, methodically prepared, and systematically perpetrated by the most pedantic dogmatists that ever existed." Putting it more succinctly, artist Arie Galles, a child of refugees who ended up in Tashkent during the war, has called the Holocaust "a calculated, systematic commitment to the eradication of an entire people."[17] Both Jankelevitch and Galles are of course not alone in expressing these facts. Still other artists feel that the Holocaust is the most important event of the century. And, finally, some artists are religious, some are not.

Tikkun Olam

One of the interesting, even astonishing, things about the interest in Holocaust subject matter is the increasing emotional commitment to it during the last few decades. This is in part derived from the apparently never-ending sadness at the loss in lives; the constant anger over the ways people were humiliated, tortured, and then murdered; the anxious sense that the world still does not care very much or not enough—that Jewish blood remains cheap—and that, given subsequent mass murders of populations, little was learned from the experience.

Murray Zimiles (born in 1941) states the issue directly. After the birth of his first child in 1984, he turned to Holocaust themes, saying: "It became clear that I, a Jew, an artist, had to deal with the seminal Jewish event, or perhaps universal event, of our time—which is the Holocaust." On another occasion he advanced the notion that the Holocaust might be "the pivotal event . . . [in] all human history. As an artist, it is my obligation to deal with this subject." Among his favored themes are images of burning Polish synagogues (fig. 9). Sidney Chafetz (born in 1922) has pointed out two other reasons why artists have turned to this imagery. First, like others, he is shocked and upset by the efforts of the Holocaust deniers; and, second, his children consider the event to be ancient history and tangential to their lives. In response he has made a series of lithographs entitled *The Perpetrators* (fig. 7).[1]

For these and other reasons, Gerda Meyer-Bernstein, who witnessed Kristallnacht as a child, insists:

> Now, more than ever, is the time to document the Holocaust. . . .
> In the 50s and 60s, people were still afraid to face the Holocaust
> head-on, afraid to confront the suffering, brutality, and murder.
> My entire life has been focused on human rights violations
> because of the oppression and cruelty I experienced as a child
> in Nazi Germany. In my art, I want to confront people bluntly,
> forcing them to deal with their feelings and attitudes about the
> Holocaust.

As the Holocaust recedes into memory, she wants her art to be more confrontational, as if to deny the passage of time. To make her intentions as clear as possible, she has exhibited works such as *Block 11* since 1982 (fig. 20). It is an installation of about six hundred suitcases covered with the names, birthdates, and registration numbers tattooed on the arms of prisoners. Meyer-Bernstein prefers to exhibit the work in dark, claustrophobic spaces, forcing the viewer to respond directly to the piles of luggage and what they imply.[2]

Howard Lee Oransky (born in 1955), who uses documentary photographs, says: "I can't not make paintings of the Holocaust, because I can't forget that it happened" (fig. 22). The question for him is not why one should paint such scenes, but "how to find the most effective method of presentation to make forgetting impossible." And Jerome Witkin (born in 1939) believes that he does not "persist in painting Holocaust imagery, but rather 'it' persists in and through me" (fig. 26). He feels that the event did not last only from 1933 to 1945, but rather "in every moment from that time onwards, forever." He has asked (perhaps, more properly, *demanded*): "How can an imagist not paint this and not become obsessed by it?" So strong are his emotions that he has called his paintings of Holocaust scenes "my purpose in life." When trying to explain the depth of his feelings, the only language that came to him was this: "I'm saying 'fuck you' to Nazism and all that is eternally stupid and ignorant and violent in all governments and in ourselves."[3]

One obverse side to that kind of anger is a close and sympathetic identification with the victims. Few have expressed this as strongly as Ruth Weisberg (born in 1942). In 1971 she published a set of nine prints with an introductory essay entitled *The Shtetl: A Journey and a Memorial*. The images include one of a burning synagogue, from which a woman flees carrying a bundle on her shoulder. In other prints groups of people stand and/or mill about, a sense of apprehension foreshadowing the imminence of death, which will come to all members of the community, or aged Jewish men, wearing their prayer shawls as scarves, walk past old, dilapidated buildings. About the people she portrayed, caught halfway between boredom and fear, she wrote: "I am a branch, a resting place for their souls. This book is my life's journey in place of theirs." Later she so described all of her art (fig. 29).[4]

In this respect her thoughts parallel those of such poets and novelists as Emily Borenstein and Julie Salamon. In Borenstein's "I Must Tell the Story," a poem about the death of Jewish people in Warsaw, from her book *Night of the Broken Glass* (1981), she writes,

Names pile up like pebbles on tombstones.
To forget you is to let you die twice.
To forget you is to hear forever blasting in my head
the single long note of the Shofar sounding in the houses of the
dead.

And this passage from *White Lies* (1987) by Julie Salamon, a child of survivors, articulates a feeling similar to Weisberg's: "Those Jews aren't nameless, pitiable beings to me, yesterday's swollen bellies, a 40-year-old newsmagazine cover. They are my mother, my father, my uncle, my aunts, my cousins. They are me."

One, of course, does not have to be an artist to express identification with the victims. This is borne out by a project initiated in 1993 by Meg Levine (born in 1963), then a graduate student at the University of Colorado. As part of a Holocaust Awareness Week, she conceived the *Boulder Holocaust Remembrance Project*. First she designed and built a large ceramic piece composed of the word REMEMBER arranged in three parallel tiers. In the lowest tier three of the letters had slots in their tops as if they were ballot boxes. She then collected responses to the question How Does the Holocaust Affect Your Life? and had them placed into the slots. Among the responses was: "I feel as if I'd been killed there, too." Of the faces seen in a book about survivors, one visitor wrote: "I see those faces and love them. They are my face. I am theirs."[5]

Sympathetic identification shades off to the more general notions of witnessing and memorializing. Miriam Beerman, who has painted close-up images of tortured victims lying in pools of blood, says quite simply: "There are those who feel they have to bear witness, and I happen to be one of them." Daisy Brand (born in 1929), a survivor of several camps including Auschwitz, also insists on acting as a witness: "One of the principles underlying my work is the wish to give testimony to an era, and communicate an experience that is totally unique in history and which I was a part of" (fig. 18). And Alice Lok Cahana (born in 1928), who survived Auschwitz, Guben, and Bergen-Belsen, has said that even if there is no language to describe such horrendous experiences, she must still tell or visualize the events that she witnessed (fig. 19). This is essential so that those who died will not have died in vain, especially now because of the Holocaust deniers.[6]

Each artist has his or her own reasons for using Holocaust imagery—personal memory, identification with the victims, the desire to bear witness, the need to keep public attention focused on the event, the hope of creating images that might help prevent such an event from recurring, and the wish to link the Holocaust both to oppression in other countries and to marginalized peoples (women, homosexuals, and ethnic and religious groups) in any or all combinations. Several artists have said that their motivation also derives from the secular Jewish sense of social obligation and responsibility, and a surprising number have directly invoked the mystical cabalistic notion of *tikkun olam*, the spiritual/religious version of secular obligation.

In cabalistic literature, the concept of *tikkun olam* marks the final stage of the creation of the universe and assigns the role of responsibility to people. During the creation itself, cosmic disturbances occurred. One interpretation holds that a certain amount of divine light was caught and placed in special vessels. The light was so strong, however, that the vessels burst and the light poured out, evil elements then mixing with divine ones. As a result, in the words of Gershom Scholem, the great historian and interpreter of cabalah, "The restoration of the ideal order, which forms the original aim of creation, is also the secret purpose of existence. Salvation means actually nothing but the restitution, re-interpretation of the original whole, or *Tikkun*, to use the Hebrew term."[7] Or, variously, people are responsible for restoring harmony, striving for the perfection of the world and mending its defects, in effect, recapturing the spilled divine light.

Weisberg states her point of view very succinctly:

> What I do feel very strongly is that my desire to make art, to create meaning, and to be generative is a conscious commitment I make to being affirmative in the face of the knowledge of great systematic cruelty and inhumanity. To remember and to affirm have for me a specifically Jewish sense of renewal. It is the part I can play in the repair of the world—*tikkun olam*.

Mirit Cohen (1945–1990), a child of refugees, who grew up in Israel before coming to the United States in 1975, invoked cabalah directly when, referring to her art, she said that her "visceral desire to mend the broken 'glass' [the broken vessels] and to build bridges with electric wires [a modern update] has been the search for the impossible."[8]

Renata Stein, who was born abroad, acknowledges the importance of cabalah as well. She has said: "The cabalists have been saying that we have to create a world if our world has been destroyed." To express both destruction and re-creation, she uses found objects and fragments. "Joining together broken pieces of rather humble origin into new configurations—and thus a new reality—is an act of *tikkun olam*, of mending the world and our broken spirits." And by using cabalistic imagery, she hopes her art will light in others sparks of inspiration and hope.[9] Unlike Newman, whose stripe paintings of the late 1940s assertively symbolize the beginning of the universe, Cohen and Stein, more temperate and moderate, not to say modest, locate their art at the end of the process of creation, in the repair necessary to complete the wholeness of the world.

Edith Altman (born in 1930), who experienced Nazi brutality in her native Germany before leaving that country in 1939, and who is a student of Jewish mysticism, offers the clearest visual statement of the mystical aspects of *tikkun olam*, particularly in a performance piece she created in 1986 entitled *When We Are Born, We Are Given a Golden Tent, and All of Life Is the Folding and Unfolding of the Tent*. The tent, made of canvas and painted a golden color, contains silhouetted figures of herself and her father, who was interned for a short while in Buchenwald and deeply scarred by the experience. She created the work after his death.

She has carried the tent to various cities in this country and in Europe, and has sat in it with Germans, Poles, and Jews, as well as Americans, in order to speak about "the pain of the past that we shared." Like a shaman who wants to heal herself and others, Altman hopes to draw into the tent God's presence for direction, healing, and for transforming the shared pain. As she has indicated: "As I fold and unfold my tent, I hear my great-grandfather telling my father, who then told me, that the work of the cabalist is to repair himself or herself and to work toward the repair of the world—to bring it back into balance."

The tent, then, which is not a fixed structure, is a symbol for building temples "within ourselves to house the spiritual presence during our nomadic wanderings through life." Part of Altman's own search for *tikkun olam* is, as she said, "trying to face a personal dark as well as the darkness felt by other people." As a result of her study of cabalah, Altman believes that "everybody has a function. I see mine as healing. The idea of *Tikkun*—which means repair—is part of cabalist thinking."[10]

In her more secular moments, Altman feels that remembering the Holocaust is at the heart of her work and that she feels she must memorialize those who died. Gene Fellner, whose mother was a survivor, in part memorialized her experiences, particularly in a series completed in 1984 entitled *A Train Full of Children*. He hoped that it might allow us to "feel what my mother went through [and] it if can make us feel that horror deep down inside of us where we don't often like to venture," then maybe it might also provoke us to help make the world a safer place in which to live. Using Holocaust imagery, he believes its lessons "can help teach us to look through our own eyes and our own hearts and never abdicate to any government's policy, to patriotism, or to fear."[11]

In similar fashion Pearl Hirshfield, who has made reconstructions of concentration camp entrances, feels that her art "centers on the outrages I feel when confronted by the inequities and brutalities of society, whether local, national, or global. Judaic tradition has always emphasized the role of the Jew as being of help to those in need, regardless of who they were. In the present climate we seem to be losing this part of our heritage." She is all the more insistent, therefore, in feeling that her "art carries on the tradition of the Jewish conscience" (fig. 27). Marty Kalb (born in 1941), who uses documentary photographs among other sources, feels compelled to offer his "work as a protest against the insane acts of the past as well as a warning against insane acts of the future." There is a great need, he believes, to reach people, to strengthen their resolve, and to support the social fabric.[12]

No doubt all the artists would agree with Hannelore Baron (1926–1987) when she said that "as an exhibiting artist it is my duty to make a statement for peace" (fig. 12). Baron's sense of duty takes on special resonance because she experienced directly the brutalities of Kristallnacht in 1938. Her childhood home was ransacked, her father beaten and taken to Dachau. When she was able to return to her home shortly after, she saw her father's bloody handprints on the wall. (The family was reunited and made its way to the United States in 1941.) Of that period in her life she said: "The early formative years as a Jewish child in Nazi Germany have left a permanent imprint on my life and work. I feel I must speak out on behalf of other victims to protect their fate, and carry with me the memory of those who succumbed." Similarly Cahana, a survivor of three concentration camps whom I cited earlier, feels that "we who survived were charged by those who did not come back to tell their story, to tell what happened. It is a silent oath that we took. . . . My work cannot end with the Holocaust, but with the image of freedom and hope. With the survival of the human spirit."[13]

Tikkun olam, indeed! But in the context of the Holocaust, there is another side to *tikkun olam* and to the sense of Jewish social responsibility. That is, artists both feel and say not only that they think these are Jewish qualities, but that they enact them almost defiantly precisely because they *are* Jewish. Artist Galles believes that even if art cannot express the full horror of the Holocaust, abandoning the attempt would grant Hitler his victory: "Each survivor must individually affirm our humanity and existence" (fig. 28). And author Michael Lerner also holds that Hitler would ultimately triumph "if the Jewish people no longer testify to the possibility of the transformation of the world."[14]

However much artists invoke the idea of *tikkun olam* to meliorate senseless violence in the world, and however much they want to remember the dead, there is at the core an anger that will not go away. I keep coming back to this because it seeps in around the edges of conversations and reverberates through my correspondence. Although sometimes the anger is quite apparent, often it is subsumed by the desire not to hate but to help others; or it is even miraculously suppressed, as with

Cahana. She has said that if she hates, then she has been contaminated by Hitler's germs. She steadfastly refuses to pass on that kind of hate.

Thus, the anger lives somewhere in the emotional space between, say, these lines from the Reform prayer book for the High Holy Days: "And how unyielding is the will of our People Israel! After the long nights, after the days and years when our ashes blackened the sky, Israel endures, heart still turned to love, soul turning still to life," and this passage from philosopher Vladimir Jankelevitch's *Pardonner?* (And Should We Forgive Them?):

> We think about it during the day; we dream about it at night. . . . This agony will last until the end of the world. . . . We can at least *feel* unexhaustedly [*sic*]. . . . This is our 'resentment' [*ressentiment*]. For *ressentiment* can also be the renewed and intensely lived feeling of the inexpiable thing; it protests against a moral amnesty that is nothing but shameful amnesia. . . . Forgetfulness here would be a grave insult to those who died in the camps and whose ashes are forever mixed with the earth.[15]

On Biblical and Mythological Imagery

There is basically no continuity between the war and the immediate postwar generations on the one hand and artists who came of age in the 1960s on the other. Images and approaches to subject matter favored by figures such as Lipton, Rothko, Ben-Zion, and Shahn are, for the most part, not continued by younger artists, who are much less inclined to present their subject matter in biblical, mythological, or traditional imagery. And it does not seem to matter if the artist is a survivor or a person born years after the end of the war. Nevertheless there are at least two artists (there must be others whom I have not located) whose work connects comfortably with that of, say, Ben-Zion and other earlier artists. These are the American-born (1924) George Segal and the Czech-born (1929) Tibor Spitz.

Segal, like some other artists, had been reluctant to work with Holocaust imagery. He rejected "the whole idea of dwelling with death." Others, equally averse, knew, however, that sooner or later they would have to confront the Holocaust in their work, and waited either passively or hopefully for the right moment to do so—a casual conversation with a friend, a trip to Eastern Europe, the death of a survivor parent. With Segal the moment came when, returning from Tokyo in 1982, he saw reports of the Israeli invasion of Lebanon on American television. "I was horrified," he said, "for the first time in my life to hear anti-Semitic words tumbling out of the tube. . . . In that moment, I decided to do the Holocaust piece."

Segal had been asked to design the piece in question, *The Holocaust* (1983), for a site in San Francisco overlooking the Golden Gate Bridge, by the Committee for a Memorial to the Six Million Victims of the Holocaust, but he had delayed giving his decision. Now, as part of his research, he studied documentary photographs of the camps taken immediately on liberation. He was struck, as he said,

> by one single horrifying fact. The German determination to kill the Jews. . . . The one visual hook I uncovered was the arrogant contempt displayed by the Germans in their chaotic heaping of corpses. In any culture, if a human being dies, there's an elaborate, orderly ritual that accompanies the burial . . . , and if a modern state turns that order topsy-turvy and introduces this kind of chaos, it is an unthinkable obscenity. I determined that I would have to make a heap of bodies that was expressive of this arrogance and disorder.

But, not wanting only to reproduce German savagery, Segal posed the "corpses" so that both a six-sided star and a cross became apparent in their overall configuration. Further, a woman holding an apple lies with her head on a man's abdomen, who in turn has his arm on the central figure, invoking images of Eve, Adam, and God. Among the figures there is also a young boy protected by an older man, suggesting Abraham and Isaac as well as the persistence of civilized values in an uncivilized situation. The Eve figure suggests regeneration and survival, also exemplified by a single figure standing near a barbed-wire fence, the only standing person in the entire composition. Segal has combined documentary images with biblical themes, and has provided the viewer with ways to respond other than sheer horror.[1]

Tibor Spitz's experiences of the war were radically different from Segal's. The son of a cantor and a schoolteacher, Spitz and his family survived the war in Slovakia, living for a time in a hole dug out of a hillside in mountainous forestland near the town in which he was born. Approximately seventy relatives were murdered before the war ended. After the war his situation improved, but anti-Semitism remained a constant during the many years of Communist rule. Trained as an engineer, Spitz turned to art after escaping to the West in 1968, living at first in Canada for almost a decade before settling in the United States. Without a continuous, sustaining community to fall back on, Spitz has invoked in his art combinations of memories of the war, family history, and traditional imagery as in *March to Eternity* (1983) (fig. 6). It includes a monumental Jewish male wearing phylacteries as he prays over the corpses of his coreligionists while an endless number of others trudge off to their certain deaths.

Of such works, Spitz has said that "pictures of the long lines of people with hounded faces moved from my tortured past to the canvases. The empty spaces they left behind were replaced by [the] memory of them. Maybe this way the agony they have been through has not been totally in vain and forgotten. My pictures somehow try to keep them alive." In addition to his desire to witness and memorialize, he also wanted to show the "unbroken spirit of the persecuted, [their] dignity even in a situation facing a certain death . . . , but also looking far ahead into the future with perfect confidence of survival."[2] One imagines that despite all of Spitz's anguished memories and experiences, of remembering dead relatives but at the same time realizing the fact of his own survival, the presence in the painting of the traditionally dressed and shawled Jew at prayer is an affirmation of the Hebrew slogan: *Am Yisroel Chai,* the people of Israel live!

Spitz has made other paintings, including a torso of a bare-chested biblical prophet weeping to heaven and a bearded Jew in old-fashioned clothing clutching a Torah while surrounded by flames, which recall works of earlier artists. On the other hand, he links himself to more contemporary imagery in a work entitled *Anguish and Pain,* which shows the head of man in profile behind prison bars, his teeth clenched, obviously in great pain. This work resonates with those by most contemporary artists who choose not to use biblical or mythological themes, and therefore do not link themselves with such artists as Rothko, Ben-Zion, and Ben Shahn.

Pier Marton, a video artist born in France after the war, has said:

We live in a world that tries to protect itself from its own
shadow. It is, in part, our desire to run away from 'problems'
that allowed the massacre of the Holocaust to take place. If in

my work I use any kind of imagery or sounds reminiscent of the Holocaust, it is its directness that will move me to it. The desire to shock myself and others into confrontation with what most of us would prefer to live without represents the hope for a cathartic transformational awakening.

He goes on to say that both mythology and the Bible are not as well known today as in the past. "Television and its raw data approach . . . is the mythmaker of today. People seem to respond more strongly to the documentary approach than to, say, the story of Abraham and Isaac. Why use some mythical approach when Holocaust survivors are still among us? They are the loudest and closest Holocaust imagery I can find" (fig. 41).[3]

Kalb agrees, finding that contemporary viewers know less about mythology and the Bible than those in the past, and therefore cannot make appropriate connections between such imagery and the Holocaust (fig. 24). He feels that such works need translations:

Most people are not prepared to read the symbols and to see the connections between Biblical and mythological content and current personal experience. Add to that the obvious differences that derive from ethnic heritage, and the problems of communicating meaning are magnified. A direct graphic representation of an incident can usually transcend the barriers of communication.[4]

Zimiles, Oransky, Anna Bialobroda, and Witkin feel that biblical and mythological imagery simply lack proper impact. Zimiles says:

The subject requires force, not myth. The artist must confront the viewer in an unambiguous way. He must show the horror, the pain, and the loss. The image must be the vehicle that propels the viewer into a world of undeniable recognition of what happened fifty years ago.

And then, setting off the events of the 1940s from the continuum of history, he adds, "The Bible and western mythology are the glory of our civilization. The Holocaust is the shame of the inheritors of that civilization."

Oransky feels that because the experiences and memories of the war were still so raw in the 1940s and 1950s, artists could not directly confront either documentary photographs or realistic Holocaust imagery. Now, decades later, Oransky finds no need of mythological or biblical imagery, "since right here on earth the Germans made manifest for us what massive, unrelenting, inescapable suffering and despair look like. . . . For me, any introduction of myth or drama can only serve to reduce the horrible reality of the Holocaust, so I avoid it" (fig. 22). So, too, does Bialobroda, a child of survivors, who finds that such imagery distances the viewer from the Holocaust, which for her "is actual, here, real" (fig. 21). Witkin says simply and starkly: "An indirect or symbolic image seems now to lack the confrontation needed to portray the Holocaust" (fig. 26).[5]

Chafetz, for whom the perpetrators are just as real (fig. 7), says that in confronting the Holocaust's "torturous reality," he found the politicians, industrialists, soldiers, bankers, and their foreign allies to be the "vicious, evil, murderous individuals who initiated it. They were monsters. But they weren't mythological beings. . . . In my belief, the Holocaust wasn't something visited upon the Jews by some god-like being; it was the direct result of a plan instigated and carried out by immoral humans." For this reason he created a rogue's gallery of portraits of about forty individuals, to show what they looked like—which was just like other people.[6]

For some the issue is a more personal one. Grace Graupe-Pillard has said that since the late 1960s she has been concerned with the marginalized. It occurred to her that she was working through personal fears and anxieties based on family stories about loss and suffering (fig. 35). Consequently her connection to the Holocaust grew more existential and psychological than religious or even historical. And because of the availability of information, she found that she was able to deal more directly with issues that confronted her "without the need for symbolic bridges." For her: "After the Holocaust, a belief in God was impossible— biblical or mythological imagery feels remote and dead." Susan Erony (born in 1949) says that she feels no spiritual, emotional, or intellectual connection to mythological or biblical themes. Museums have been her temples instead. She finds that she cannot treat the Holocaust metaphorically. Rather: "I need to directly refer to it in order to give it its due" (fig. 42). This need led her to include, in her first Holocaust pieces begun in 1989, photographs of camps, of Jewish cemeteries, and

German steel plants in order "to give a sense of place, to address the fact that most of the Jews in Europe are in graves, and to approach the relationship of industry to militarism in the Third Reich." Destroyed Jewish culture is her overriding theme.[7]

That these artists do not turn to biblical and mythological images might mean for some an impoverishment of possibilities. But one might argue instead that the uniqueness of the Holocaust demands new types of responses that cannot be incorporated into older themes or into an ahistorical biblical time. Rather, these Jewish-American artists much prefer to cast their images in real or historical time. Yet the issue is not so easily polarized, since even though many artists ignore the biblical past, they invoke the concept of *tikkun olam,* an organizing principle within Judaism, obviously a point of reference dependent less on subject matter than on an attitude of mind that remains within a Jewish context, and a mystical one at that (see "Tikkun Olam," this volume).

One might argue, then, that a traditional attitude has in part substituted for traditional images even among artists who ignore the biblical past, a carryover of their Jewish heritage and background. But once the artists finally internalized the notion that the Holocaust could only be experienced as the supreme Jewish sacrilege of all time and therefore was incapable of being mapped in archetypal fashion (which had largely faded from memory anyway), then it became possible to locate it on a different continuum of Jewish memory—the immediate, the existential, the adversarial.

In this regard Jewish-American artists arrived at the same realization that artists who were in the camps came to immediately—the Holocaust itself was the point of departure for Holocaust imagery, not the ancient past or tradition. The same was true, as James Young has pointed out, for European Jewish writers during the 1930s and 1940s: "In the diaries and poetry written during events, the ancient archetypes were steadily displaced by more recently acquired figures . . . until only the figures drawn from contemporaneous events seemed adequate to the current tragedy." Thus the Holocaust became its own archetype. Among the poets Young mentions, Yitzhak Katzenelson, who was murdered in Auschwitz, is particularly apposite. A few lines from his poem, "Song of the Murdered Jewish People," indicate his contemporaneity with artists today. Katzenelson refused to invoke biblical prophets such as Isaiah, Ezekiel, or Jeremiah, since they seemed inadequate to convey the destruction of an entire people. Rather he fastened on a single Jewish child.

> . . . Isaiah! You were not as small, not as great
> Not as good, not as true, not as faithful as he.

For Katzenelson, as Young states, Isaiah is no longer a model figure, but rather it is the ghetto children, who "are now the new Jewish standard against which all past and future Jewish suffering will be measured."[8] This immediately calls to mind that unforgettable photograph of the solitary, anonymous Jewish boy with his hands raised during one of the roundups in the Warsaw Ghetto.

Expressing the Inexpressible

No single overriding theme or image has subsumed all others as the common or typical way to depict the Holocaust, no visual shorthand enables the viewer to connect immediately with the subject. But one way to fathom the variety of images and approaches is to arrange the works in a loose chronological framework—as European events evolved—rather than when the works were completed in the United States, always keeping in mind that with a different group of artists the configuration could be quite different.

Just as there was suffering by real people, so the Holocaust was initiated and carried on by real people. At least two artists have addressed this theme, Chafetz and Arnold Trachtman. Chafetz has said that for years he had wanted to deal visually with the Holocaust but was frustrated because nothing could equal documentary photographs and motion pictures. In 1990 he decided to portray the perpetrators, not the victims; the people who, as Chafetz said, "made Hitler possible"—lawyers, educators, soldiers, industrialists, financiers, doctors, scientists, religious figures, journalists, and artists (fig. 7). By using period photographs together with biographical material, he found that he was able to combine his aesthetic and didactic interests to achieve "formal coherence and

■ 67

at the same time . . . educational impact."[1] Most of the lithographs in the series, *Perpetrators,* are portraits, but there are a few informal family scenes, especially of Joseph Goebbels and his family.

Chafetz carefully refrained from either glorifying or demonizing his subjects, which is what makes the cumulative impact of the images (about forty) so frightening, and ultimately so chilling. These are ordinary people (who look like ordinary people) who gained control of a country and then proceeded to brutalize, enslave, and murder entire populations. The banality of their appearance belies the consummate evil of their activities, and so Chafetz leaves the viewer with such questions as How could they? Why did they? Is this what evil people look like? Is this the guy across the street?

Trachtman has also painted industrialists, politicians, and others who contributed to Hitler's rise. Beginning in 1985, he started to paint multifigured and multipaneled works that have the look and feel of skewed photomontages. One work, for example, *Peace in Our Time* (1991–1992), consists of three panels, one on top of the other. The top one includes British prime minister Neville Chamberlain, surrounded by well-wishers at a news conference, holding the treaty to which he and Hitler agreed after their meeting in Munich in 1938. It was on that occasion that Chamberlain said: "Herr Hitler has repeatedly expressed his own desire for peace and it would be a mistake to assume that these declarations were insincere." In the middle panel, Jews are forced aboard a train, and the bottom panel consists of an enormous stack of eyeglasses taken from prisoners before they were murdered in the gas chambers. Two small insert panels in the top register include German dive-bombers and an aerial view of factories.

Another panel, *The Jewish Passion with Donors* (1989), is in the form of an inverted crucifix. In place of the traditional donor portraits, Trachtman has included industrialists such as Krupp and the chief of I. G. Farben, Karl Krauch. The central panel includes the core Nazi group, Hitler, Göring, Goebbels, and, in the top panel, are chimneys haloed by the phrase, *Arbeit macht frei,* the slogan placed above the entrance to Auschwitz (which several artists have incorporated into their works). Trachtman makes these works, he says, to fight the dangers of apathy and forgetting. And his desire to include portraits is, like Chafetz's, to demystify to whatever extent possible the Holocaust and to see it in terms of human agency. That is, whatever were the circumstances that caused the Holocaust, it was certain individuals who inaugurated or helped inaugurate it, who carried it out, and who profited from it.[2]

To make portraits of important German figures and then to confront their visages in an exhibition is, I suspect, easier for Jewish Americans than for Jewish Europeans. I would also suspect that the kind of internalized self-hatred European Jews have absorbed from their environment is less common, or at least less evident, among American-born Jews. It is not surprising that Jewish Americans in search of ancestral roots have memorialized, mythified, and sentimentalized the shtetls and ghettos of Eastern Europe by wrapping them in bittersweet nostalgia derived from novels, short stories, and family reminiscences. Certainly artists who came of age after 1960 are not embarrassed by these places and see no reason to repress them in their visual imagery. They no longer fear searching for roots other than American ones, especially since both the physical and temporal distances are so vast and unbridgeable that such places are no longer real. This in no way lessens the impact of the art of those who create shtetl scenes. If anything, whether the works are documentary re-creations or imagined scenes, they make the loss all the more tragic by providing the viewer with a visual sense of what was lost, and help keep in the mind's eye the places our parents, grandparents, and so on called home.

Ruth Weisberg, for whom the Holocaust is this century's central event, was among the first of her generation to use any sort of Holocaust themes, and specifically shtetl imagery. Her memorialization of the shtetl in her book *The Shtetl: A Journey and a Memorial, Text and Nine Original Prints,* published in 1971, no doubt, reflects Weisberg's own sense of mourning for the lives that will soon be taken and a future that will never occur. Altogether the scenes add up to an appropriately sad vision of a way of life that no longer exists.

Eleanor Antin, an artist who, like others, has been both discovering and inventing her Jewish memory, has made at least one motion picture and one installation set in the shtetl. Although she does not, as she has said, "frontally address the Holocaust," what haunts her "is the loss of the rich Jewish culture of Eastern Europe. That loss, and the need to invoke it, are at the core of my Jewish works. Without that past, we have the blandness of suburban Jewish life." Compared to "that dismal desert," she much prefers the "noisy, dense history" her mother passed on to her of the East European community. Her mother, an actress in the Yiddish theater, ran several hotels in the Catskills, one of which catered to elderly East Europeans, and it is from this cultural milieu that Antin's "Jewish" pieces are generated. They evoke images of both actual exile and of imaginative re-creation in which, as she says, "time collapses into itself as layers of life fold over and under each other in the uneasy symbiotic relationship of memory and history."

The phrase "symbiotic relationship of memory and history" is not just a figure of speech for Antin. In some ways her approach is similar to that of the American Scene painter Thomas Hart Benton, whose work is as different from Antin's as night from day; both entered into the lives of their parents and re-created aspects of those lives as if they were their own.

In Antin's ninety-eight-minute film *The Man Without a World* (1991), set in a shtetl and concerned with the struggle for "a dignified life [that countered] poverty and racial hatred," she used old-fashioned acting styles and filmic techniques. One could therefore imagine that one was watching a movie made in the 1930s or earlier. Of it she said that she had wanted to "enter the lost world of the past from the inside, not to stand outside of it and see it as history. . . . In a sense I am conceiving the past as a foreign country and an old film as a 'foreign film,' which an audience can enter and experience, but with a sense of the distance they have traveled to get there."

Her *Vilna Nights,* a video installation, traps any sense of nostalgia the work might have had in the immediacy of the shtetl's imminent destruction (fig. 8). The viewer looks through a bombed-out wall into a courtyard. One sees across a courtyard a building wall punctuated by three windows and in them glimpses of the lives of the now vanished inhabitants—an old tailor, a woman burning a letter, and two terrified, abandoned children imagining a Hanukkah feast. These scenes are projected by video discs onto the three windows. Sounds of various kinds waft through the devastated courtyard.[3] The viewer is looking at nothing less than the physical extinction of a culture, its living quarters, its people, their lives. There is nothing to contemplate other than that sense of loss, of relatives one might have had, of an existence one's family might have led in other, earlier times. The emptiness remaining is apparent and appalling. Depending on how close one is through age and knowledge of one's relatives' experiences in the shtetl, one feels truncated at some deep emotional level. It is not as if one wants to say, I could have been there if my parents or grandparents had not emigrated. Rather, the feeling is that a past you did not even know you had has disappeared. There is a profound sense of loss for a vital culture you will never be able to experience.

The paradox of trying to recover images and experiences of a community's past as it is being destroyed is very much a part of Murray Zimiles's work. But the engine that drives Zimiles is rage rather than remembrance. In his *Holocaust Series,* begun in 1986, and in his *The Book of Fire,* completed in 1991, which consists of twenty-two lithographs and three woodcuts with texts consisting of eyewitness accounts of atrocities, Zimiles describes the barbarous treatment of Jews (fig. 9). *The Book of Fire* begins with scenes depicting the *Aktion* carried out by German university students on May 10, 1933, against books considered un-German in spirit and tone. Other individual works both in *The Book* and in the *Holocaust Series* show brutalities committed against helpless individuals—such as the old and women and children.

The principal part of *The Book* is given over to works showing the burning of wooden synagogues. These buildings, in Zimiles's view,

> reflected the epitome of the carpenter's art. Craftsmen using folk-architectural tradition, combined with the ecstasy of trying to please God, produced some of the most beautiful wooden structures ever erected. [During a trip to Poland] I searched for them throughout the towns where they once stood only to find emptiness and martyred cemeteries. This became my subject, my passion, my mission, and my obsession—how to convey that loss.

For Zimiles the loss was not just in the buildings. He wanted "to show the destruction of the greatest folk art ever done by the Jewish nation [and] by implication also try to show that the tradition and the artisans were erased along with the architecture." His project was to show nothing less than the disappearance of the central artifacts of a culture—its houses of worship and all that they contained.

In the thematic development of these works, he first used photographs, but then realized, as he said, that he had "to invent images that did not exist in the photographic literature." By "invent," however, he did not mean to add "Fiddler-on-the-Roof" motifs or symbolic forms redolent of ghetto nostalgia, but rather images of people being violated by German soldiers and their allies as well as people fleeing from their burning synagogues.

Zimiles toured Auschwitz during his visit to Poland. He described what he saw and how he felt in an extraordinarily moving letter to his son. He describes how he found the sight of piles of shoes heartbreaking. "I feel so overwhelmed by the futility and stupidity of the barbarism committed against these innocents. The anger in me is immense." He goes on to describe how the old, the young, and the pregnant were delivered directly from the trains to the ovens. "Who were these people who could do such a thing?" he asks. He decides that he will never return to Auschwitz.

> I don't need to. I can take the walk I just took in my mind and soul. I now realize that something made me start the Holocaust series, something I can't yet understand. . . . It's my way of telling him [in this part of the letter Zimiles refers to his son in the third person] what happened to my people and for him to respect the five thousand years of history that I inherited. Just maybe he will understand and feel pride in that force that has kept his people alive. And so, my son, my feelings are for you and I am now weeping for all the children like you who couldn't understand why they weren't allowed to grow up. And for the parents who held them as the gas choked them. Imagine the sense of failure, of outrage, at being unable to save your child.

Perhaps Zimiles's most startling image, which has appeared in both painted and print form, and which might have been created as a response to his visit to Auschwitz, is that of a man—head thrown back and shrieking at the heavens—carrying a six-pointed star around his neck, as if a crown of thorns had slipped onto his shoulders. The not-so-silent scream of the Jew wearing *his* badge of martyrdom around his neck is as much Zimiles's as it is that of the uncountable parents who perished, knowing that sense of failure and outrage in the gas chambers.

Murder and terror were obviously not confined to the camps, since Jews were often killed wherever they were found, most insistently in the most devout Christian countries. Poland, the Baltics, and Slovakia had the highest ratios, according to one source—90 percent in Poland and the Baltics, 89 percent in Slovakia.[4] One is reminded of these statistics by Judith Goldstein's *The Burning Barn* (1995) (fig. 10). Born in Vilna, Poland (now Vilnius, Lithuania) and a survivor of several camps after the Vilna ghetto was destroyed, she painted this work based on a friend's story of how 1,040 Jews were rounded up and burned to death in Krivitz in Poland.[5] (Members of my wife's family had a similar experience, but not a similar fate, when at the last moment a German officer opened the door of their synagogue in Govorovo in Poland just before the timbers of the blazing building crashed down on those inside.)

Such barbarities as these and the ones Louise Kramer records in *Kaunas, Lithuania: Women and Children Rounded Up, Told to Undress, Then Marched to the Death Pits and Shot* (fig. 11) were commonplace in Poland and other Eastern European countries. As indicated in this sculpture, seemingly part of a dismembered frieze, the cries, screams, and pleading of the subjects gained them no sympathy. Other sculptures by Kramer have similar themes and titles: *Auschwitz: Women and Children Told to Undress and Line Up for the Showers, Sent to the Gas Chambers Instead, Treblinka* (1994), *The Four Hanged Women*. In these works some figures appear emaciated and skeletal; some mirror infinite sadness and numbed fear; others moan and cry. The historical record shows that survival was a matter of purest chance—a bullet missing its mark, a gas chamber out of gas (I once heard such a story).

All these works were made after 1987, when Kramer, asked for a drawing for a book on war and death, turned to Holocaust themes. Since her husband, a German Jew, spent his terror-filled youth until 1938 in Nuremberg, Kramer was certainly familiar with stories of Nazi atrocities. And like most other artists exploring these themes, her intentions are twofold. On the one hand, she works, as she says, "toward moving the onlooker to feel, experience what occurred under Hitler," and it is true that her works are among the most viscerally conceived, the most physical of these artists. On the other hand, because of "my people's profound wound," she feels that scrutinizing the Holocaust is a task "whose ultimate intent is appreciation of life." It boils down to a very simple statement of belief: None of this should ever happen again.

Kramer has also said that "to depict the women and children faced with torture, gassing, and death, I had to allow some of the terror to fill my body."[6] Other artists have reported similar responses, and even though they obviously could not duplicate the stomach-turning sense of fear of the victims, they nevertheless became aware of their all-consuming dread, not as a verbal abstraction read somewhere but as a physical presence within their own bodies. I mention this to make the point that some artists are capable of turning this kind of identification into something different and *lesser*—to use this kind of language to explain something in their lives that has little or nothing to do with the Holocaust, or to confuse, willfully or not, the terror of the Holocaust with personal anxieties far removed from the European situation in the 1930s and 1940s.

For example, Jonathan Borofsky (born in 1942) incorporated Holocaust imagery into his work in the late 1970s. On one occasion, describing a work, he mentioned that he dreamed "that some Hitler-type person was not allowing everyone to roller skate in public places . . . , the oppressed figure holds a symbol of the universe showing that spirituality is endangered along with life itself." Borofsky evidently decided in his dream to assassinate this figure because it meant that a controlling element was restraining him. He has included a Hitler-like figure in some works to illustrate this dream. And in 1979, just after Borofsky had written about this dream on a gallery wall in preparation for an installation exhibition, a person named Todd Gast introduced himself to the artist. Borofsky asked, " 'Gassed' as in ovens?" Gast said no, and explained that his last name, *Gast,* means "guest" in German. Since Borofsky had included an oven in this exhibition, he wrote "gast means guest in German" on the oven.[7] If Hitler was invoked in regard to some personal sense of restraint, and Borofsky seems to have had no qualms in doing so, then exactly who and what, on some kind of sliding scale of terror and personal experience, could the victims of the Holocaust invoke in their dreams? The reduction of Holocaust imagery to visualize a personal problem seems to me to be as pitiful and reprehensible as the playful wording written on the oven.

By contrast, Hannelore Baron was neither as interested nor as willing to reveal her private thoughts (fig. 12). Even though she had gone through Kristallnacht, she did not want to call attention to herself as a victim, but rather to project in her work "a strong feeling and identification with the Jewish victim." She revealed little more than to say that her collages were "meant to be a form of document attesting to events I cannot forget," which included social injustices wherever they might have happened. Her small assemblages of paper and wood appear to be quite fragile, and suggest time's ravages and, more important, secrets hidden behind their closed and boarded-up surfaces. As in the work of so many camp survivors and children hidden during the war, allusion replaces description (whether in conversation or in art)—the memories too horrific to confront directly, let alone reveal in public. Only Baron knew what lay behind the sealed spaces of her collages and assemblages.[8]

Those hidden during the war often literally lived in sealed spaces. These spaces are recalled and recorded in several paintings completed in 1992 by Kitty Klaidman (born in 1937), who survived the war with her family in Czechoslovakia. An artist for more than thirty years, Klaidman did not make paintings based on her experiences until she revisited the area of her childhood in 1990. There followed in quick succession at least five series, which she termed "a visceral response to the ghosts of my past." *Black Forest Memories* (1990) invokes the flight through the woods to the storeroom beneath the attic of a village farmhouse, where the family lived for two years. These experiences are explored in *Hidden Memories* (1991–1992). Simultaneously Klaidman painted *Childhood Revisited: Homage to Jan Velicky,* the man who saved the family, and soon after, she completed *The Past Purged* and *The Family Book.*

The series *Hidden Memories,* of which one work is reproduced here, is about hiding (fig. 13). Titles include "Trap Door," "Crawlspace," and "Dark Corner with Window." An area of light appears in each work, which Klaidman feels represents the existence of people like Jan Velicky, who essentially kept the family alive, and also the fact that her immediate family did survive. By not giving the architectural elements a sense of solidity and density or a strong material presence, Klaidman made of the attic a space for the mind to wander through. She also left the spaces empty to indicate that they were intended originally as storage areas, but, for her, areas charged with emotions of fear and hope, hate and love. As with Baron's collages, only so much is revealed, and no more.[9]

On the other hand, Philip Orenstein (born in 1938), who was hidden by a French farm family near Paris, avoids specific narratives concerning his childhood, preferring instead to create works concerned with the occupation and liberation of France. These are incorporated into a series of very large works, roughly eight by twenty-two feet each. Like others for whom the Holocaust is part of their autobiography, Orenstein repressed his experiences until recently, even though they were neither more nor less brutal than those encountered by other French farm children—but with the caveat that if he had been caught, he would have been killed.

Images of black crosses and airplanes appeared in several of his works in the 1970s, but it was not until 1988, when he visited the sites of his youth, that he conceived of his large-scale project. For the then forth-coming fiftieth anniversary of the liberation of Paris, he wanted to exhibit a group of works in the Salle de Fête in the eleventh arrond-issement in Paris, the district in which he was born and in which many Jews had lived. For a variety of reasons, the exhibition was held instead in 1994 in Houdon, the rural farm town where he was hidden.

The works contain both personal experience and public memory (fig. 14). The format often resembles graffiti that Orenstein saw all over Paris in 1988. Generally one or two large images dominate each work. In the *Fall of Paris* the Venus de Milo, symbolizing the French love of clas-sical civilization and rational thought, confronts Hitler, who represents war, destruction, and irrationality. Juxtaposed against them (and around the large figures in the other works) are small graffitilike figures of flags, photographs of family members and famous public figures, wall writings, and names of places. Each painting is like a wall imprinted with Orenstein's memory images as if applied over a period of time, a palimpsest of private and public issues, occurrences, and events. Other works in the group include *The Battle of Britain; De Gaulle and Pétain; The Vel d'hiv Roundup,* for the *Vélodrome d'Hiver,* where Jews in Paris were taken before being sent to the death camps; *The Battle of Stalingrad,* included because, according to Orenstein, when the French realized, after the Battle of Stalingrad, that the Germans were going to lose the war, they began to treat Jews better; and *The Liberation of Paris.* The only extended personal note occurs in *The Vel d'hiv Roundup,* in which printed passages describe how a cousin the same age as Orenstein was caught in a roundup and sent to his death.[10]

Millions of others were not so lucky—to have survived or, a half century later, to be able to attempt to incorporate their experiences into the larger history of the war years. Instead they were forced into the trains and sent to the murder and labor camps. Several artists have focused on this aspect of the Holocaust, some exploring images of train tracks as metaphors for a great range of themes, and others on the means of transportation, the cattle cars.

For Elyse Klaidman (born in 1960), the Holocaust is both family and public history. She began to use Holocaust imagery after traveling to Czechoslovakia in 1990 with her mother, Kitty Klaidman. "I had heard countless stories," she has said, "about those years, but until that trip I had been unable to integrate them into my own feelings and life." More recently she has painted large landscape scenes "as a metaphor for the contradictions I have confronted in my explorations . . . , the paradox of beauty in wretchedness, the physical beauty of a sunset behind the gates of a concentration camp, or the geometrical forms created by the destruction of trees and homes."

A work that contains both specific and symbolic elements, *The Tracks* (1993), contains a fence post, barbed wire, a track, and two crossties (fig. 15). Mostly blood red in color, the painting may also refer to the fact that the grandfather of Klaidman's husband was known to have died on a transport near the end of the war. (One of his grandsons recently tried to find the exact place where his grandfather might have been buried, and did come upon a small marker where sixteen people had been interred.) Perhaps, then, the Star of David that appears in the configuration of forms in the painting allows it to become both a private and a public memorial for all those who perished along the way. As Ori Z. Soltes, director of the B'nai B'rith Klutznick National Jewish Museum in Washington, D.C., has suggested: "This most anonymous piece of God's earth—track, post, wire, dirt—is bursting with personalized anguish."[11]

Debbie Teicholz, like Klaidman a child of survivors, has also included train tracks in her Holocaust works (fig. 16). The photographic triptych illustrated here includes ploughed furrows flanked by tracks. The central image was photographed in Israel and the tracks in Budapest. The connection to the Holocaust is not direct but rather one of inference and association, and suggests that disparate forms and associations might unexpectedly trigger Holocaust analogies in an artist's imagination. Of this work Teicholz has said:

> As I smelled the rich, amber rows of Israeli earth, I thought about the rows of train tracks, and I still hear the silent screams. I walk through life with a displaced step, meaning as I walk here and there in 1996, my mind was really thinking of them and how come? Therefore, I chose the triptych, the three-panel form, to bear witness to the rhythm of the past-present time warp in which I travel daily.[12]

There are two thoughts in Teicholz's last sentence. Bearing witness is one, and easily understood. The second, "the past-present time warp," is different and more complicated—relating to Lawrence Langer's observation that camp survivors often live in both durational and chronological time. Teicholz obviously does not have camp memories, but she does imply that through her family history the Holocaust is ever present in her mind, and its presence can make itself felt at any moment, that it is lodged in her psyche never to leave or to be exorcised, a kind of second-generation "durational time" experienced by children of survivors. (Wendy Joy Kuppermann is, as has been seen, another example.)

In Teicholz's phrase, she creates "traumatic remnants." The image— a painting, a photograph, an installation—can externalize her feelings and give them some kind of visual shape, which then reduces, if for a moment only, their overwhelming impact. Some artists whose families were not directly affected by the Holocaust have said that to this day they still weep when reading about the Holocaust and even weep when creating their works. These do not take place in "durational time," but they do indicate the profound depths of feeling the Holocaust still provokes in people, how contemporary it still is, and how burdensome its memory, direct or indirect, can be.

Wendy Joy Kuppermann (born in 1958) has also photographed train tracks as well as intentionally quotidian views of the camps. In the photographs that make up the series *The Far Country*, begun as a result of an unexpectedly wrenching visit to Poland with her parents in 1989, the intended thematic concerns are not always evident (fig. 17). This is purposeful, for in photographing "the machinery of genocide, the nuts and bolts of bigotry, intolerance, and inhumanity," Kuppermann points out that this is what it looks like—simple, familiar forms in the environment, the commonplace physicality of objects associated with places of genocide—which then force one to grapple with the incomprehensibility of the Holocaust, an extraordinary event that took place in ordinary surroundings. That is, the photographs of various locations in and out of the camps tend to look neutral until they are placed in context. The distance one has to travel between the banality of the scenes (but not the banality of the photographs, which are carefully calibrated for maximum effect) and the horrors of the Holocaust crosses a terrain of unimaginable, even impenetrable terror. For example, the loss of detail in the upper part of the accompanying photograph corresponds, as we know from our vantage point, to the loss of control of one's life, of one's future, as one proceeds down the tracks to the point of disembarkation in one of the camps. In effect, we are at once there with the victims and witnesses to their imminent death.

Kuppermann has stated that she avoids titling her works because as a child of survivors she had to

> fill in the blanks to my parents' fragmented accounts of life in the camps and to interpolate my own horrified vision of family and personal narrative into all Holocaust footage I encountered, most of it immeasurably more graphic and traumatizing than any of my own still images. . . . I want you to ask unanswerable questions. I want you to people the barren landscape as your imagination sees fit. I want you to "fill the blanks" as I have had to. I want to stimulate you to engage with the work on intimate, even cathartic terms.

This presupposes a sympathetic viewer, one emotionally ready to imagine what the train tracks signify—as with the sound of the trains in Claude Lanzmann's film *Shoah*—and a viewer ready to deal with the incomprehensible actuality of those commonplace train tracks—with what they uncommonly represent.

In another photograph in this series, Kuppermann shot a view at a camp of a now derelict set of train tracks passing between two severely foreshortened wire fences and guardhouses. The implied narrative suggests that the tracks represent the possibility of freedom of movement until that moment when the vanishing points converge in the distance and the fences merge, bringing any sense of movement along the tracks to a screeching halt, a stunning and abrupt metaphor for life and death in the camps.[13]

By contrast Daisy Brand, who began to use Holocaust imagery in the 1980s, creates images of tracks, endless halls and passages, and what appear to be burnt Torah scrolls in immaculately rendered porcelain, earthenware, and wood assemblages (fig. 18). She uses porcelain in part because it is a material that must be fired and therefore recalls the crematoria. But in her works fire creates rather than destroys. Her works elude precise meaning and are, in effect, her private musings on her memories, but she hopes to evoke emotional responses in the viewer.

She has said that her pictures

relate to some of the lasting impressions I have of scenes on
the way to the camps, railways, buildings and interiors. The
black, gray, and orange color of the night sky in Auschwitz, the
stripes of the prison uniforms, for example, are all part of the
imagery. At the same time I am trying to avoid renditions of
actual scenes or events. I am hoping for the mood and symbol-
ism of the work to communicate its meaning.

Epilogue (1994), illustrated here, refers to the endless hours spent after
liberation sitting in train stations on the way home from the camps, as
well as to the ruins of the lives of the survivors, the "desolation and loneli-
ness." She adds: "Most significantly, there was no sense of joy to be free
in that immediate aftermath of the war."[14]

We cannot question her desire for privacy or what seems to be her
intention to control potentially nightmarish memories by the elimination of specific objects or details. I would speculate that her works represent a desire to confront and at the same time to deflect memories of
the Holocaust. It might be that in aestheticizing them they are tamed in
some way, and thus prevented from overwhelming her. I know a survivor of Auschwitz who related the following story to me. Toward the
end of the war, when she was about thirteen, she and her mother had
to march barefoot on a winter evening through the snow to another camp.
Her mother, ill and exhausted, fell down. She stopped to help her
mother, but a guard ordered her to keep walking. He said that he was
going to kill her mother and would kill her, too, if she remained. Her
mother told her to keep walking, to live as long as she was able. The
young teenager had to make a horrible choice—stay with her sick
mother and die or abandon her sick mother and live. At this point in the
story, she broke off her narrative and told me that what she remembers
most about that night was the full moon, that its light streamed beau-
tifully through the trees, and that the landscape was gorgeous. She
had to remember the moment in a way that would allow her to live with
its memory, and so she aestheticized it to make it tolerable.

I do not know if Brand in a similar manner acknowledges and then
masks her experiences, but it is a point to consider. It is a point relevant,
as well, to the work of Cahana, who also survived the camps. She
turned to Holocaust themes after a trip to her native Hungary in 1978,

when she realized that no memorial existed to honor the Jews murdered during the war and that nobody in her hometown remembered her mother, who had died in Auschwitz. She then decided to create works memorializing not only her own experiences but honoring such figures as Raoul Wallenberg. Her earlier lyrical abstractions, influenced by Morris Louis, gave way to images that now recalled her wartime memories (fig. 19). Titles included *Arrival, Arbeit Macht Frei, Sabbath in Auschwitz,* and *Pages from My Mother's Prayerbook.* Yet, despite the change in subject matter and even in the way she now scratched and tore a painting's surfaces, her washes of color and the splashing of pigment provide a sheen to her works that masks the sense of horror that motivated them in the first place. The tension between aesthetics and memory provides a deeply moving poignancy.[15]

The in-your-face attitude of Gerda Meyer-Bernstein, who witnessed Kristallnacht, is totally opposite that of Brand and Cahana (fig. 20). In fact, Meyer-Bernstein's installations are among the most materially aggressive of all Holocaust-related works. (Her themes also include atomic destruction, apartheid, civil wars in Third World countries, and the Vietnam War.) As she has said, "I work with a vocabulary of intense personal forms." Or, at least, beginning in the early 1970s in a series of works honoring Raoul Wallenberg, she contextualizes forms in an intense personal way.

The Wallenberg works are made up of photographs of Nazi activities attached to blankets and other surfaces. By the 1980s she began to make three-dimensional works, including an homage to her grandfather that included images of her grandmother placed on a tabletop, a man's portrait centered in a six-pointed star, and a book about the Gestapo. These, in turn, gave way to installations with such titles as *Requiem* (1983) and *Shrine* (1991), which include such objects as German helmets, barbed wire, memorial candles, and photographs of crematoria, and, as in *Block 11,* piles of luggage.

On the suitcases Meyer-Bernstein has painted names, birthdates, and concentration camp numbers, including those of her immediate family, which serve her "as the umbilical cord in the death-birth cycle. Through my children and their children's children, there is invincibility and continuity of the life cycle." As much as the suitcases celebrate the continuity of the Jewish generations, they also commemorate death. For Meyer-Bernstein luggage was "the one personal thing these people had left at Auschwitz, and then that was taken away from them. Suitcases are particularly interesting to me because we all carry around our psychological baggage. They move us from place to place. You put some of your best belongings in them." She explicitly acknowledges these feelings when she says of this particular installation: "When I take them [the suitcases] down, I actually go through a mourning period. When it's rebuilt, it's like a rebirth."[16]

Bialobroda, a child of survivors, who began to explore Holocaust imagery around 1980, has also incorporated suitcases into paintings that explicitly suggest departure and loss. And she has painted piles of shoes (like the piles of objects taken from crematoria victims that can be seen at Yad Vashem in Jerusalem and at the Holocaust Memorial Museum in Washington, D.C.) in a room flooded with a luminous light (*Still Life,* [1989]). This particular work is especially compelling because the piles initially look as if they might be bushes, thus provoking a sharp recoil once it is realized how shockingly easy it is to turn a horrendous theme into a pleasant visual experience. Like Kuppermann, but in her own distinct way, Bialobroda mediates—on that thin line—between the banality of forms, how we might view them and the context in which we must place them.

Her *Violation* (1986) is equally mind chilling (fig. 21). As Bialobroda has explained, it is based on a description quoted in *Shoah* of a truck designed more efficiently to gas prisoners, the exhaust fumes from the engine being piped into the rear of the truck. The description is dated June 5, 1942. One part reads:

> For easy cleaning of the vehicle, there must be a sealed drain in the middle of the floor. The drainage hole's cover, eight to twelve inches in diameter, would be equipped with a slanting trap, so that [body fluids] can drain off during the operation. During cleaning, the drain can be used to evacuate large pieces of dirt. The aforementioned technical changes are to be made to vehicles in service when they come in for repairs.[17]

In Bialobroda's painting one sees a wheel; a closed rear door with its shut grille; the other, opened door, which allows us to see the killing space within the truck; and the drain, so matter-of-factly described in the report. What seems at first glance like an arrangement of geometric forms is in reality an enclosed area where thousands of people were murdered.

Bialobroda's soft, expressionist brushwork belies and sets off the businesslike tone of the request for a more efficient instrument of murder in an appropriately ice-cold way. A question that always arises when one reads reports like this or sees the numbers cited in the count of a week's worth of murders is: How does one deal with it? As in other similarly understated works, the psychological distance one must traverse between the forms and their real content extends the meaning of the words; "sublime terror," an aestheticizing term that serves as an imperfect but common answer.

Bialobroda has also included in one of her works a boxcar, an object that resonates so profoundly and disturbingly among Jews. To have been transported in one is, as Lawrence Langer asserts, "one of the primal events in the memory of so many surviving victims, the boxcar journey." Langer also discusses the point of view he calls "the cattle-car point of view," in which one viewed the world from the inside, denied any sense of freedom or choice, denying literally any point of view from which to view the world, in which there was no future, only the ordeal of the moment, a vivid symbol of closure, of imminent death.[18]

Howard Oransky, who has used Holocaust imagery since 1975, also made at least one "boxcar" painting, his *Railroad Car with Human Cargo* (1983), based on the famous documentary photograph of three women peering from an opening laced with barbed wire near the top of a boxcar. They stare out. We stare at them, separated from them by the wooden side of the car that rises high enough to block out all but their faces. We occupy the space of the oppressor and are helpless to do anything about it. It is as if one of them has shouted out, just as the train is leaving and before she can finish her thought, Dan Pagis's poem, "Written in Pencil in the Sealed Freight Car" (quoted in its entirety):

> Here in this carload
> I, Eve
> with my son Abel
> If you see my older boy,
> Cain, son of Adam,
> tell him that I

Oransky has also painted those who died in and those who survived the camps. *Will These Bones Live?* (1990–1994) is one of several works he has made of camp inmates (fig. 22). The left panel is entitled "Arrival of Two Women at Auschwitz-Birkenau"; the central one, "Crematorium at Buchenwald; the Vision of Ezekiel"; and on the right, "Liberation of Two Men at Wobbelin." In other, similar works, figures are emaciated but not skeletal, and often stare at or face frontally the viewer. In explaining his method, Oransky says that he starts with documentary images:

> I figure the best way for me to establish a link with the viewer is to get at one portion of one image, one moment of emotional recognition with one individual. . . . This kind of emphasis [holds] a greater potential for establishing a dialogue with the viewer than the frequently reproduced images of piles of corpses, which although important, are like the visual equivalent of reading statistics only. In another generation the survivors will be gone. How will we remember the Holocaust? What images will be used in the construction of memories? I purposefully include images of women and men and as many age groups as possible in my work.[19]

His concern for the unique individuality of each victim—both a painful and a defiant response to the impersonal mechanisms of German repression—is shared by other artists. As Langer has stated: "Before their physical oppression, Germany's victims were deprived of power and ousted from any social bonding that included them as objects of mutual concern." Then, hunted down and herded into boxcars, they were systematically stripped of their individuality. Shorn of their hair, tattooed, they lost their names and any important identifying physical and psychic characteristics. By emphasizing their individuality, Oransky contributes to the validation of the self in a camp culture that denied the uniqueness of the self.[20]

This triptych, *Will These Bones Live?*, presents some interesting questions concerning belief: How seriously do Jews read the Bible? How much is read as history? How much as received faith? How does one weigh Judaism as a cultural construct or a religious belief system? Do Jews trust God after the Holocaust? Do they even believe in such an entity? These questions prompt either-or or both-and answers. Oransky apparently falls into the both-and category. Under the central image with its dead—or possibly still living—body not yet cremated, Oransky added the text from Ezek. 37: 1–11, which prophesies the resurrection of the dead in the valley of dry bones. But he consciously omitted the remaining verses of the chapter (Ezek. 37:12–28), which prophesy the return of the resurrected to Israel, where they will live in everlasting peace. If the Jews survive, Oransky seems to be saying, they will do so without God's help and intervention. They will endure and flourish by virtue of their own strength and achievement. But, like other artists, Oransky here uses language and biblical imagery with which many Jews still feel culturally comfortable despite their apparent lack of faith in the deity.[21]

In an interesting variation on the central panel of *Will These Bones Live?*, Oransky in 1995 painted *Auschwitz Gate: The Testimony of Rudolf Hoess* (the commandant of Auschwitz). It reveals a landscape of train tracks entering the camp. Above the roof of the long, low building, Oransky has superimposed on the sky the following lines from Hoess's memoir: "The stench of burning flesh was carried for many miles and caused the whole neighborhood to talk about the burning of the Jews." In a panel added to the bottom of the painting, in the space earlier reserved for the verses from the Book of Ezekiel, Oransky includes more of Hoess's text. This totally secularizes the spaces for biblical prophecy seen in *Will These Bones Live?* One might even argue that by associating Ezekiel and Hoess as he does, Oransky could be suggesting that God and the Jewish people have an adversarial relationship similar to that of Hoess with the camp's prisoners. Or, to put it differently, we know where Hoess was. Where was God?

Mindy Weisel, born immediately after the war in Bergen-Belsen, arrives at a similar impasse in her *Who's the Driver?* (1984) (fig. 23). She began the work by writing about destiny and fate. "My anguished question asked over and over: 'How did the Holocaust happen, where was God, and if there is no God, who is the driver?'"[22] One reads her words in the painting as seemingly going up in smoke, that they will be lost forever, that nobody will read them or hear them spoken. The image of words burning has a special resonance for Jews that reaches back into history beyond the crematoria. For as Renata Stein, another artist, has said, she uses Hebrew letters in her works in response to the legend of Rabbi Chaninah, who, as the Talmud states, was burned alive by the Romans for insisting on studying with and training students when he was prohibited from doing so. While he was burning at the stake, his disciples asked him what he saw. He replied that he saw parchment burning and the Hebrew letters rising to the sky, forming new prayers.

Since, according to the Talmud, these are letters from the same alphabet that made up the Ten Commandments and the Torah, which God gave to mankind, they are immortal and indestructible and will re-form into words once again. By extending this belief into the post-Holocaust era, so, too, the Jewish people are considered to be indestructible and will re-form themselves as a group in the immediate future. But where Stein hopes her art will generate in others sparks of inspiration (*tikkun olam*), Weisel, using suggestive Jewish imagery, expresses her doubts.[23]

Marty Kalb, who began using Holocaust imagery in 1988, also seems to be a both-and person. As he has said:

> I was raised in a nonreligious but culturally aware Jewish environment. . . . Though my knowledge of Judaism is limited to basics, I am confident that my work is motivated by and encompasses many Jewish themes. Examples would include sanctity of life, the belief in personal responsibility, the belief that good will triumph over evil, and that education and the knowledge of truth will enable humanity to make the world a better place.

Motivated by secular Jewish humanitarianism, as well as by the concept of *tikkun olam,* Kalb (whether he realizes it or not) offers his work "as a protest against insane acts of the past as well as a warning against insane acts in the future."

Like Oransky, Kalb has painted camp scenes as well as scenes of synagogue desecration, murder by roving execution squads, and portrait close-ups of dead bodies. For dramatic effect he prefers to juxtapose abstract elements against images based on documentary as well as personally taken photographs (fig. 24). To the factual material he collects, he likes to add spiritual elements:

> When I am selecting [materials], I am looking for something else, something beyond the details of the incident, which suggests to me the possibility that I might confront the viewer with a universal message. The effect might be an emotional connection between the facts portrayed and the viewer's sense of humanness. The final work should as well portray issues of remembrance and homage.

They No Longer Cry (1993) combines abstract images based on photographs of a survivor and a pile of bones, which are centered between non-objective, coruscated surfaces of paint, as if to imply that the images hidden in the end panels are too terrible to contemplate. For, as Kalb has said: "The Holocaust was an evil unique in the history of humanity's vilest behavior."[24]

Reclaiming Jewish Selfhood

Like Kalb, Oransky, and other artists, we all know that the Nazis tried to destroy the identity and personality of every Jew, whether in or out of the camps, and that the attempt to reclaim their selfhood is difficult but not always impossible. As Israeli novelist Aharon Appelfeld has observed, the Holocaust seems so completely unreal that it needs to be brought down "to the human realm," not in the sense of simplifying the way it is understood or of glossing over its horror, but in trying "to make the events speak through the individual and in his language, to rescue the suffering from huge numbers, from dreadful anonymity, and to restore the person's given and family name, to give the tortured person back his human form, which was snatched away from him."[25]

Few have done this more intently than Aharon Gluska. When visiting the archives at Yad Vashem, he happened on photographs of camp inmates and obtained copies of many of them. He wondered who these people were, shorn of their hair and clothing, and what their names were. In 1995 he was able to connect some photographs with names after discovering information in the museum at Auschwitz. But then came the question of how to present them (fig. 25).

Gluska's technique is to apply black paint directly to a photograph, as if in a private ritual, and then wipe away patches of paint "to expose and 'rediscover'" the faces and identities of those depicted. He then places a glass over the photograph, which acts as a barrier to remind the viewer that looking directly at the face in the photograph "is not the same as understanding what it was like to live (and die) in that time." Gluska then paints on and wipes the glass, leaving the eyes of the subject largely untouched and therefore brighter than the rest of the face. Finally, he stretches silk over the glass, which forces the viewer to place him- or herself directly in front of the photograph, eyeball to eyeball, as it were. In this way the viewer must confront each subject individually. A room full of such portraits, then, does not appear as an extended group portrait, but rather as a roomful of single portraits of solitary individuals.[26] Gluska's altered photographs provide a sepulchral imaging to Roland Barthes's observation that the effect a photograph had on him "is not to restore what has been abolished (by time, by distance), but to attest that what I see has indeed existed. . . . Photography has something to do with resurrection." Gluska's work seems a meditation on Barthes's notion that in comparison to realist painting, a photograph "is not a memory, an imagination, a reconstitution . . . , but reality in a past state, at once the past and the real."[27]

By contrast, Jerome Witkin prefers to make figurative paintings based on his own imagination rather than on documentary photographs. And his imagination has led him to the creation of images of torture and death in several works in his cycle of Holocaust paintings, begun in 1979—*Death as an Usher: Germany 1933* (1979–1981), *Terminal* (1987), *Liberation 1945* (1989); *Beating Station and After, Berlin 1933* (1989–1990), and *The Butcher's Helper, Buchenwald 1941–45* (1991–1992). *Terminal* and *Liberation* are easy to look at, but the others are not. The former shows a reasonably well-dressed man, wearing a yellow star on his jacket, sitting in a boxcar whose door is open. The latter presents a kneeling inmate, his back to the viewer, praying in front of a crumbling stone wall.

The first work in the series, *Death as an Usher,* is in the form of a triptych, which Witkin associates with paintings of martyrs. The year 1933 in the title is meant to suggest "a seedy, dirty, filthy, corrupt Germany." In the first panel, reading from left to right, a brown-shirted arm holding a gun reaches diagonally into the picture space toward the head of a girl wearing a yellow star who is crouched over a dead man sprawled on the street who also wears the star. She appears transfixed, screaming a silent scream. To her right two women, terrified, flee. The middle panel shows one of the women running into the door of a theater. In the third panel an usher with Hitler's face shines a flashlight on the now-dead woman who is being dragged off to the right by a human dressed in sheep's clothing. In effect the Holocaust has begun. "We see," as Witkin said, "what the running girl sees. She moves between the reality she's leaving and the still crueler reality she's entering, the prophecy of the Final Solution. . . . We go from light to darkness, from panic to hysteria, from unseen gunman to the smiling usher that is Hitler."

The violence in *Death as an Usher* is only a prelude to the fury Witkin depicted in *The Beating Station and After,* an eleven-foot painting of a scene in a dim basement where prisoners are beaten to death. When asked why he makes works like this, Witkin admitted that he did not know, but commented: "I have a need to open heavy, dark doors; this is the heaviest and the darkest." He probably said this before he completed *The Butcher's Helper,* a work of even greater violence (fig. 26). The left section (not in the accompanying illustration) shows naked and blindfolded prisoners being tortured. The remaining part shows American soldiers arriving too late to stop the tortures. Behind them, naked bodies hang upside-down from meat hooks. To the right two camp guards have just finished raping (and cutting off the limbs of) two women. This painting, twenty-nine feet long, was created, Witkin said, "to hold the viewer inside an unavoidable scene." The scene, or one like it, must have been in Witkin's thoughts for a few years, because in an interview in 1991 he said: "Jewish law is based on the mother's blood, the mother's line . . . [and] women are about longevity, by their possibility of giving birth. With this in mind, the women used to be more violated sexually, cosmetically, more violated by experiments to their bodies."[28] Whatever else one might say about this work, it is about female mutilation, and it provides a shockingly vivid visual analog to literary historian Andreas Huyssen's observation: "After we have remembered, gone through the facts, mourned for the victims, we will still be haunted by that core of absolute humiliation, degradation, and horror suffered by the victims."[29]

The Butcher's Helper comes as close as possible to internalizing and identifying with the agonies of the victims, their unendurable pain, and their torment. And we ask: For what purpose did they suffer such outrage? In the end their agonies and deaths have no ultimate meaning. They did not die as martyrs who chose death rather than renounce their beliefs or their religion. The German intention to kill every Jew made such sacrifices and martyrdoms irrelevant because no choice was involved. By emphasizing the sadistic aspects of those experiences, Witkin reveals their baseness and purposelessness. His rage parallels that of Lawrence Langer, who, after discussing the literature of Auschwitz, wrote:

> There was no rein on the shame, humiliation, and torment
> that the Germans could inflict on their prey, no check to their
> malice, brutality, lust for ruin; their talent for atrocity was
> unlimited. . . . [The victims] were nullified, not sacrificed;
> murdered, not martyred.[30]

Witkin does not construct a narrative of survival or heroism—just an account of death from which no moral can be extracted, no rationale fathomed, no lesson learned, no martyrdom honored. Just plain straight-out murder, repeated six million times.

It is a truism that only survivors fully understand the wartime Jewish experience, but at least one American-born artist has tried to suggest what camp experience must have been like. Pearl Hirshfield has made at least three installations in which, as one walks through them and listens to the recorded sounds, one can imagine and feel in one's body, obviously at a great physical and psychological distance, what prisoners encountered. They are *Shadows of Auschwitz* (1989), *Shadows of Birkenau— Zur Desinfektion* (1994), and *Verordnung!* (1994). In simulating the look and feel of the camps in the first two works, Hirshfield helps the viewer barely begin to understand, in Lawrence Langer's trope, the difference between durational and chronological time.

Although *Shadows of Auschwitz* has been exhibited in slightly different forms (depending on the configurations of the available space), the installation includes an entrance, marked "Eingang," though which one walks down a long, narrow corridor suggestive of a boxcar (fig. 27). Throughout the piece walkways are confining in order to suggest the claustrophobia associated with the herding and caging of the victims. One sees written on a wall a quote from Primo Levi's story "The Coin": "Beyond the fence stand the lords of death and not far away the train is waiting." One passes tall wooden fencing, barbed wire, and planks containing mirrors with tattoo numbers written on them. At the exit one sees one's reflection covered with tattoo numbers. All the while searchlights move back and forth.

The first tattoo number one sees is Primo Levi's. Others have been added to the piece as Hirshfield meets or is contacted by survivors. She inscribes each name on a scroll and keeps them in a phylactery pouch. However, the first numbers one actually sees on entering the installation are those of the Jaworzno-Chrzanów train that was bound for

Auschwitz when it was derailed by partisans. Hirshfield has said that she wanted to commemorate that as well as many other unrecorded acts of heroism, and this provided her with the opportunity to do so. She has also included the names "Bieli" and "Nissenzohn," her parents' surnames, on the fence. All the names are important because a central purpose of the work, according to Hirshfield, is "to give back dignity and identity to those victims."

Her *Shadows of Birkenau—Zur Desinfektion* literally explores the same terrain. In a nine-by-eighteen-foot space, a fence bisects the work. On one side the fence is painted to suggest brick chimneys outside the crematoria. On the other side naked electric bulbs and exposed wires hang along the walls, which also contain collaged photographs of victims. The exit corridor, lit by a red light, has one mirror on the wall with the sign ZUR DESINFEKTION, which reflects the viewer as well as the bricks and ovens within the crematorium.

Verordnung! is a tribute to Emmanuel Ringelbaum, the archivist of the Warsaw Ghetto, whose journals were found in milk cans after the war. The installation includes large milk cans flanking a glass case placed against a wall hung with copies of documents from the ghetto. On the floor in front of the case are bricks and a manhole cover, referring to the sewers, which were pathways of communication and escape. Excerpts from the diary are heard, relating activities—roundups, deaths, and so on—of daily life in the ghetto.[31]

During and certainly toward the end of the war, the Germans tried to hide the existence of the camps. Arie Galles found captured Luftwaffe photographs in the National Archives Cartographic Branch in Washington, D.C., that document the existence of the camps as well as evidence of the desire to eradicate them from memory. He calls his set of drawings based on these photographs *The Fourteen Stations Suite*. They are "Auschwitz/Birkenau," "Babi Yar," "Buchenwald," "Belzec," "Bergen-Belsen," "Gross-Rosen," "Dachau," "Chelmno," "Treblinka," "Mauthausen," "Maidanek," "Sobibor," "Ravensbruck," and "Stutthof." A fifteenth drawing, "Khurbn Prologue," is based on an aerial view of Belzec before the construction of the camp. (*Khurbn* is Hebrew for destruction.) Galles considers these works to be his Kaddish, and his memorial to those who died in the camps. Their title *The Fourteen Stations* is deliberate. Like the other artists, he is opposed to all forms of intolerance, but he wryly observes that many of the same people who honor another Jew crucified some two thousand years ago nevertheless think that fifty years is more than enough time to mourn and then basically forget the Holocaust:

> The cross or crucifix is displayed in thousands of houses of worship, in sculpture and painting, craft and literature. . . . Yet, after only fifty years, Jews should lay to rest the memory of millions of martyrs, and not disturb the world with the memory of their martyrdom, or with the remembrance of the earthy hell that was the Holocaust.

His particular Via Dolorosa—his Fourteen Stations of the Cross—passes through fourteen camps.

A Singular Holocaust

I want to raise an issue here that is only obliquely suggested by Galles's observations—an issue that irritates several acquaintances of mine and perhaps bothers Galles as well (though he had the courtesy not to say it as baldly as I will). Those who argue that enough is enough are considered in the same category as, say, people from country X who claim that they suffered considerably during the war, and that therefore war memorials in that country should honor all victims. No Jew would deny that many millions suffered and were killed and deserve to be honored, but Jewish people tend to detect a hint of anti-Semitism when there appears to be a determined refusal to acknowledge the special circumstances of Jewish suffering during the war—that is, the German desire for total annihilation of the Jews, which was aided by any number of nationals of other countries.

According to Galles, his drawing of the site at Chelmno, illustrated here, is based on a photograph taken in 1942 (fig. 28). He found it strange that the photograph was taken at all, since there were no important military or commercial developments in the area. He surmised that the Germans wanted to see if camouflage effects were successful at the site in the Rzuchowski Forest where 360,000 Jews and 1,500 Poles had been killed. The clearing in the foreground was the site of the burning pits and later the crematoria. The long horizontal line marks a mass grave more than six hundred yards long, which was filled with personal possessions, bones, and human ash. (Galles is quick to note that the charcoal used for the drawing is also made from ash.)[32]

How does one represent the deceased? One might stay close to documentary sources, as Ben Sederowsky did in *The Scream* (1995), a work painted on a paper bag from a supermarket. But some artists have found other means to do so. In 1987, Ruth Weisberg completed *The Scroll*, ninety-four feet in length, a work based on the Torah, her own experiences, and on contemporary events (fig. 29). It contains narrative elements concerned with creation, revelation, and redemption. In the last section, on redemption, Weisberg juxtaposed an endless number of concentration camp uniforms hung on clotheslines against a distant view of Jerusalem, combining images of the victims' entirely hopeless present with their virtually hopeless vision of the future.

But what if an artist sees no glimmer of a brighter future, no comforting vision of what might be, but rather an end point to life, the termination of the present in nothingness? That seems to be the vision of Selma Waldman in her *Falling Man* series (fig. 30), composed of about three hundred drawings, begun in 1960 and completed a few years later. (Waldman is probably the most prolific artist of Holocaust-related images.) Based on the shattering experience, when she was in Berlin in 1960, of seeing Erwin Leiser's film *Mein Kampf*, which includes scenes of dumping emaciated bodies of victims into mass graves, Waldman attempted to capture the effects not of specific bodies but, as she says, of "archetypes of the unspeakable that would suspend the moments of 'falling' and transform them into 'icons of genocide'—both particular and universal." Aware that by forgoing immediacy of effect, she ran the risk of losing the connection to the Holocaust, Waldman was nevertheless willing to skirt generalization for intensely moral reasons. Since she had not experienced the Holocaust herself, she could not in good conscience make what she considered to be inauthentic works based on photographs or films. These would by "disrespectful to the dead and to [the] survivors" as well as to artists who had directly experienced the camps.

During the years she made the *Falling Man* series and until 1972, she also worked on other series and subseries made up of hundreds of drawings, including the multifigured compositions of *Das Ringen um Brot* (the struggle for bread), based on passages in Elie Weisel's *Night*, in which the author describes how starving people fought each other for scraps of bread thrown into the boxcars on the way to the camps.[33]

Israeli-born Natan Nuchi has created works that are also obviously Holocaust related and which also have universalizing qualities (fig. 31). I find that his figures exhibit some of the qualities of a predeath trance. Floating in a nonenvironment, or in a space in which the physical environment is no longer present for them, stripped of every possible defense, they seem beyond experiencing pain or even their own death. They are emotionally or perhaps already physically dead. As Donald Kuspit has observed, Nuchi's paintings are about "the human encounter with, even immersion in, Nothingness. . . . Nuchi's Jewish nude is neither a survivor or a victim, but the embodiment of moral meaninglessness." As other artists might show or suggest how Jewish people were killed, Nuchi shows how they might have felt—or really no *longer* felt—during their last moments, stripped of everything, abandoned by all.

Nuchi began in the early 1980s to make paintings with figures that reminded him of camp inmates. Aware of documentary photographs of naked, emaciated people, he saw them embodying both private and political qualities. Their nakedness and emaciation reflected their vulnerability and mortality, and, at the same time, attested to the violence inflicted on them by governments and groups of people. It was these images of suffering that Nuchi, as an artist, wanted to represent. In his mind they were still "the truest, most enduring and most honorable approach to the Holocaust in art," especially since for him "the victims, rather than the survivors, represent the essence of the Holocaust."

But in portraying victims, Nuchi ran into a moral dilemma: "I have had to contend with the morality of using the suffering of others to make art, and the relevance of making paintings in relation to the existing photographs." His response was embodied in his belief

> that the vitality of the memory of the Holocaust depends on the possibility of renewal, and metaphysically speaking, I saw my paintings as commentary and the photographs as Scriptures. I believe that paintings, when at their best, have the ability to externalize feelings and reveal an existential layer that is not apparent in most photographs, and I also believe that art can fuse and absorb the documentary materials—the visual and literary, and open up an emotional and intellectual relation to the Holocaust that the documentation does not allow.

Nuchi tests his belief when he speculates on which image would carry stronger emotional power: a photograph of Jesus on the cross or the cruci-fixion scene in Matthias Grünewald's Isenheim Altarpiece, a photograph of people being executed or Goya's *The Execution of the Third of May*.[34]

Other artists as well have made their commentary on Scriptures, and mourn for both the victims and the survivors. In fact, images of mourning are the norm; there are very few, if any, celebratory works by Jewish-American artists. At least I cannot find paintings or sculptures that show, say, child survivors playing soccer in Israel or partisans blowing up train tracks. Public memorials might in one way or another commemorate such concepts as human aspiration or triumph over evil to provide some sort of closure on the Holocaust, but Jewish-American artists do not exult. The most relevant work I can find, although others must exist, is one of the most famous Holocaust works by an American artist—*World War II*, by Audrey Flack (born in 1931)—but it is a work about survival rather than one of celebration (fig. 32).

Knowing that sooner or later she would have to confront the war and the Holocaust, she made a painting of Hitler in 1963–1964 and then *World War II* some twelve years later. Until that time, she said, she had never seen a painting dealing with the Holocaust—which, given the fact that so few were created, let alone exhibited, is a reasonable claim. She knew that she did not want to paint corpses, because there had been enough "killing and bleeding and rape" of Jews. If she made another such work, she felt that she "would be adding to the mutilation." Instead, she chose to base her central image on Margaret Bourke-White's famous photograph of just-liberated inmates posed behind a barbed wire fence at Buchenwald. In the lower part of the painting, she included some words by Rabbi Nachman of Bratislava (born in 1772), one of the intel-lectual giants of early hasidism, concerning belief in the presence of God as a means to mitigate despair. In a glaring contrast Flack placed around the former prisoners bright-colored pastries, a blue butterfly, a red candle, and a blue jar in order "to tell a story, an allegory of war . . . of life . . . the ultimate breakdown of humanity," and to include violent con-trasts of pure evil and "beautiful humanity . . . [of] opulence and depri-vation." The overall effect was shocking at the time the painting was first exhibited, but over the years several women survivors have told Flack that in the camps they would imagine a crumb of bread to be a rich pastry or that they pretended to have their Sabbath silverware with them.

Flack's contrasts, as recent research among women survivors has also pointed out, were, evidently, entirely appropriate.[35]

Most Jewish-American works are about those who died, however. In certain sculptures such imagery takes on the qualities of a monument because of its three-dimensional bulk, its sheer physical presence in a public space, and its impersonality. Sol LeWitt's *Black Form Dedicated to the Missing Jews* is such a work, large and impersonal, even though he personally wanted to memorialize the death of Jewish people in the Holocaust. It is a rectangular form made of black cinder blocks. LeWitt was invited in 1987 to create a piece for the Münster (Germany) Museum. He proposed two pieces, a white pyramid and a black rectangle, but selected the latter. "For some time," he says, "I had felt that I wanted to make a statement concerning the lack of Jews in the art life of Germany due to the Holocaust. When I saw the black form, it seemed the perfect vehicle for that kind of statement. Overt figurative subject matter did not seem adequate to the subject." Erected in 1987–1988 and placed in front of the Münster Palace, it was dedicated to the missing Jews of Münster. Demolished soon after because of much local opposition, it was rebuilt in 1989 and placed in front of the town hall in Hamburg-Altona.[36]

A very different kind of work in the general form of a monument, much more personal in intent and clearly made for gallery display and private installation, is Marlene E. Miller's *Schlafwagen: Who Will Say Kaddish for Them?* (1993–1994) (fig. 33). Miller creates Holocaust images to give voice "to that which is silenced: the victims who perished, the survivors who still cannot speak, the survivors who are now deceased." *Schlafwagen,* in the form of an architectural plinth, is, as Miller says, "a monument of remembrance to Jewish victims of Nazi atrocities." Constructed of papier-mâché, found objects, and collaged photocopied images, it includes a baby carriage containing figures writhing in agony. They lie on a wooden trestlelike structure evocative of train tracks. The carriage serves at once as a funeral cart, common in camps, and as a symbol of a boxcar. The term *Schlafwagen,* meaning "sleeping car," usually the epitome of luxury, adds a note of deadly irony. The wheels of the carriage are surrounded by ashes, shoes, and bones. Photocopies of various wartime scenes are attached to the shaft of the plinth, and around its base are unlit *yahrzeit* candles waiting to be lit to commemorate the dead (thus, the second half of the title, *Who Will Say Kaddish for Them?*). Miller answers by saying: "We the living must remember."[37]

Remembering, however, does not always need to be stimulated by specific imagery, as in Miller's piece, or by a specific commemorative intent as in LeWitt's. And so works suggestive of monuments shade off into shrines that provide a space and an atmosphere for private meditation. At least this is one of the reasons lying behind the creation of structures Tobi Kahn (born in 1952) calls "shrines," several of which he made during the 1980s (fig. 34). They shelter a small form—a flame, a human shape, a charred remnant. For Kahn these shrines "evoke ancient sacred spaces and figures that seem always to have been there."[38]

Not all were intended to evoke the Holocaust, but as a group, he considers them to be objects for meditation, objects to help create a spiritual or meditative space. Nor are they necessarily meant to pay homage to six million people, an indigestible number for Kahn, but to serve as markers for contemplating the sense of emptiness one might feel after thinking about the Holocaust, the loss of generations of victims and their posterity, the children who will never be born, the contributions to society that will never be made. These shrines are dedicated to loss as well as to the thought that we will never know what has been lost to the future.

The Representation of Loss

Let me translate these words from the general to the specific by describing four generations of my wife's family—her father's generation, hers, our children's, and our grandchildren's. The paternal side of her family, originally from Poland, survived the war in various parts of the Soviet Union and now live in the United States. My wife's father was one of six siblings who among them had twenty-one children. Those children—my wife's siblings and cousins—in turn, have and are still having children, now numbering fifty-five. And at this writing there are seventeen grandchildren. A large and largely Orthodox family, they take great pleasure in family *simchas* (celebrations of engagements, weddings, anniversaries, births, ritual circumcisions, confirmations, and graduations, among other events). My wife's mother, on the other hand, was one of ten siblings. After the war not one, or their offspring, could be found. This means that after the war there was never a family *simcha* on her side of the family or the possibility of joy taken in nieces and nephews and their offspring. She was always the sole representative of her family at her husband's family celebrations, and felt that at some deeper level, too, she was always alone at these events. If we consider that she, knowing her family had been murdered, might also have thought about contributions, great or small, her relatives might have made to society, then there is much that she might have mourned or reflected upon. Kahn's shrines, although not in and of themselves necessarily suggestive of the Holocaust, by their intention create spaces in which such ruminations might best take place.

Other artists have also taken mourning and loss in very personal directions, and have made works that are, in effect, family biographies. Based on stories her father told her, Grace Graupe-Pillard, who lost seventy close relatives, created *Nowhere to Go: The Holocaust Series* (1990–1991), a group of ten mixed-media collages of her family's travails in Europe. Each piece is contained within the silhouette of a crouching woman, whose nonspecific position might indicate that she is praying or that her hands are bound behind her back. *Nowhere to Go II—* "Family Tree" (fig. 35) contains photographs—perhaps the last ever taken—of her paternal grandparents, who were killed in concentration camps. The papers below the photographs, collaged to treelike forms, "depict their fate, complete with dates and transport notices." The *yahrzeit* candles are lit in memory of those who perished. Among the other works in this series, "Prelude to Propaganda" includes references to ethnic hatreds before the war in the form of a caricatured, hook-nosed Jewish person embracing a businessman while picking his pocket; and "Sisters," which includes photographs of cousins who survived the war hidden in Holland, dolls floating on water as if they were corpses, and a letter from an uncle and aunt who also survived the war.[39]

Works such as this begin to help answer such questions as: Who were my relatives? Can I understand the European experiences of my parents and relatives? Where do I come from? What are the connections between my ancestral and my American cultures? Do I exist in a history other than the present one? Who am I? To that extent, the process of making such works is not just about process, an ongoing aspect of contemporary process and conceptual art, but rather it can be a cathartic, healing, and psychologically centering activity. As Gabrielle Rossmer, who as an infant emigrated with her parents from Bamberg, Germany, has said about her reasons for making *In Search of the Lost Object,* an installation begun in 1991:

> I have . . . sought to understand my connection to the place of
> my birth, whose residents were responsible for the awful deed
> [the death of her grandparents, among others]. To bring BACK
> a picture of my family that was obliterated from that place
> seemed ultimately to be my task.

A visit to Bamberg in the 1970s—like Cahana's trip to her hometown in Hungary—was deeply disturbing: "We were like ghosts coming back to visit. No sign of us existed." During a subsequent visit, in the late 1980s, Rossmer proposed an exhibition to city officials of what turned out to be *In Search of the Lost Object.* The artist, for whom the installation is an ongoing project, understands both its hope and futility, since she is not certain if she is preserving, re-creating, or creating anew the lost object of the past, which might be idealized childhood memories and/or parental history. There are, she admits, very complex and indecipherable relationships between memory, intention, and expression.

Parts of the installation include a "Document Wall"—a set of sixty-six photographs of documents relating to family attempts to emigrate from Germany, to attempts to rescue family members who had not yet left Germany in the 1930s, and to Bamberg itself. Two sets of sculptures are also part of the installation—a group of forty shroudlike figures made of stiffened cloth and a set of eight ten-feet-tall hanging "garments" (fig. 36). The latter, first hung in the ambulatory of the Cathedral of Saint John the Divine in New York City, when the work was temporarily installed there, seemed to appear as angels, according to some church members, but to Rossmer "these desiccated-looking dresses are evocations of the once living." The third part of the installation, "Tablets," incorporates random personal images of Germany and of Rossmer's first American neighborhood, Washington Heights in New York City, brought up-to-date by the inclusion of photographs of the most recent waves of immigrants there.[40]

Other installation artists have used Holocaust imagery and subject matter relating to the Holocaust in different ways. Their aim is not to denigrate the Holocaust, nor to deny its centrality to the Jewish experience of the twentieth century, but at the same time not to be limited to making works only about perpetrators, victims, and survivors. Purists might object, but their objections boil down to the following proposition: There is only one way to deal with the Holocaust, and it does not include using it as a point of departure for something else. Artists might respond by saying that more and yet more of the same leads to a creative dead end as well as a removal of the Holocaust from history. That is, it cannot be considered in evolving contexts, especially by people who were born decades after the event and who have no personal memory of it or family connections to it.

Two installations, among others, test these assumptions. *From Adler to Zylber* by Melissa Gould (born in 1958) is a wall installation composed of thirty-four sheets of black-bordered white paper, each three feet square. Each contains a name and an image based on the name. "Tauber," for example, from the German word for "dove," is accompanied by a large bird of prey in whose beak there is a tiny human form. The names comes from a document that she found in a book by Nazi-hunter Serge Klarsfeld, of French Jews sent to Auschwitz in late 1942, which included, by sheer coincidence, her grandfather's name. The circumstances of his death had previously been unknown to the family. So the work in part is a memorial to her grandfather. But it also alludes to the fact that the death of these people could not be mourned properly. But what is the proper way? One way is not to limit the names to their "nameness" but to allow them to be used as points of departure for the artist's imagination, based on source material from textbooks, fairy tales, and encyclopedias. The victims are acknowledged and accorded proper respect, but their names provide a new kind of life in which the creativeness of art becomes a substitute for life itself.[41]

In her *The Anne Frank Project,* composed of two related installations, *Partial Index* (1990–1991) and *A Probability Bordering on a Certainty* (1992–1993), Ellen Rothenberg (born in 1949) found in Anne Frank a surrogate to confront the Holocaust. But she also found in her subject ways to deal with the problematics of choice in difficult circumstances, of identity, and of feminist concerns (fig. 37). And she sought ways to evoke in the viewer multiple responses to both the Holocaust and the varying ideas she brought to the works. The works, then, are not limited to the Holocaust but certainly grow from it.

Partial Index, a wooden room about forty by twelve feet, refers to the secret annex in the industrial building where the Franks were hidden from 1942 to 1944. Along one of the short walls is a floor-to-ceiling bookcase that recalls the concealed entry to the secret rooms. It is lined with a wallpaper design of photographs of Anne and her sister, Margot. Twelve doors fill the long wall. Inside are reproductions of archival materials that hang from the ceiling, interrupting the viewer's space, implying that documents, of value or not, can either guide or distract. One can also find images of pages from Anne Frank's diary and other historical documents, along with such objects as a radio or a rag that *might* have been there. These "false artifacts" offer other ways to think about Anne Frank, in human terms rather than as an abstraction. There is no logical order to the placement of these items, just as there were no reasonable choices for European Jews. Wallpaper designs on close inspection prove to be images of lice, telegraphing Anne Frank's death from typhus. There are references to Nazi regimentation and persecution, and to Anne Frank's physical presence as well as her writing. There are also specific references to her sexuality, as revealed in the most recent, unexpurgated edition of the diary, which are intended to provoke multivalent responses having to do with different aspects of the Frank family situation and of Anne in particular. Once again Anne as a human being, not as a murdered child author, is brought into the foreground for the viewer to contemplate.

A Probability Bordering on a Certainty, a separate installation that has been exhibited with *Partial Index,* is composed of particular forms that add up to a more direct, physical connection to Anne Frank. The title itself refers to the conclusion of a Dutch report, which answered in bureaucratic language a question raised about the writing of the book: Did Anne Frank write her diary under the conditions described in the book? Rothenberg chose the title because it suggests both the impossibility of being certain about memory as well as our inability to reduplicate Anne Frank's experience. To that end Rothenberg includes a false artifact, a set of business cards that state: "Anne Frank, Professional Writer," in several languages. These cards suggest Anne Frank's future had she lived. One of the most powerful objects in this installation is the "Combing Shawl," made up of the text of the first version of the diary, reproduced in the *Critical Edition* of the diary, printed on twenty-nine twenty-two by nine-inch strips of vellum coated with graphite. They are layered in the form of a gigantic cape, through which can be seen hundreds of metal combs. The piece refers to Anne Frank's combing shawl, which was found in the hiding place after the family was caught, one of the very few objects remaining of her physical presence, but which also alludes to her shaved head in Bergen-Belsen, where she died.

Another object in this installation, "Das Wesentliche (The Essence)," refers to the history of the manuscript. It consists of forty-four leather belts tightly wound around a foam-wrapped pillar. Between the belts, the foam bulges suggestively, perhaps erotically, and relates to passages (stamped on the belts) excised from the initial published version of the diary, in which Anne Frank describes her genitalia in considerable detail. Rothenberg here subsumes the innocent girl known to the public within a much more complex young woman. "By reconstituting this fully developed sense of self—including sexuality—to the lost girl, Rothenberg's work restores Anne Frank's ability to act, her agency. [Rothenberg's] is a proto-feminist Anne Frank, self-aware and self-analytical to the point of rebellion, a feisty young woman who acknowledges and seizes control of her female identity."

Rothenberg explained: "My intention in creating this work is not that of a historian or documentalist. I speak as an artist, about an experience of the diary that is personal and contemporary."[42] Rothenberg's various interrupted narrative sequences, the several allusive images, the projections into the future, and the intentional misrepresentations provoke the viewer to think of the fate and unfulfilled future of one individual caught in the Holocaust. We are to think about her from the points of view of the German authorities, of the travails of being in hiding, of the physical and intellectual remains of that individual, of her unfulfilled possibilities, and of any feminist implications that might ensue. What emerges is not a complex linear narrative but a multifaceted text about the Holocaust and some of its ramifications that has no single resolution.

Anne Frank's diary, along with the writings of Elie Wiesel and Primo Levi, all legacies of Auschwitz, are among the most best-known works to emerge from the Holocaust. The latter two authors also became famous public personalities, Levi serving in the late 1980s as the subject of a group of paintings by Larry Rivers (born in 1923). Throughout his career Rivers has turned to Jewish themes, most notably in his three-part *History of Matzah*, painted earlier in the 1980s, which is a visual history of Judaism in vignette form. The Levi paintings, however, are focused directly on the Holocaust. Based on photographs of the author, they are in effect meditations on the Holocaust, filtered in part through his experiences and observations, but without raising the sorts of issues Rothenberg explored in *The Anne Frank Project*.

Each work is dominated by a portrait bust of Levi. In one, a portrait of a survivor still in striped camp uniform emerges from Levi's head. In another, Levi is posed in front of open oven doors that reveal human bones inside. And in yet another, a camp scene emerges from his chest and fills the space around him. It includes children who wear the yellow star; there are a wire fence, barracks, and the bare indication of crematoria and rising smoke in the background. The ultimate effect is that of contemplating camp scenes through the thoughts and memories of a single person, as if in reverie. The Holocaust, although still a brutal assertion of documentary fact, is depicted with the meliorating presence of that person, softening the impact of the scenes Rivers records and protecting the viewer from the full onslaught of the historical record. His is the Holocaust quite literally with a human face, an interesting pendant to Chafetz's portraits of the perpetrators (fig. 7).[43]

Nancy Spero (born in 1926), who explored Holocaust imagery in the late 1960s, returned to it in 1990 in a work that was mediated by a literary source of a different sort as well as by a feminist perspective. It is *The Ballad of Marie Sanders, the Jew's Whore*, a wall piece that has been exhibited in various venues in the last few years. Spero put together a photograph of a bound and gagged nude woman with a noose around her neck, found in the wallet of a Gestapo officer, with the text of a poem written by Bertolt Brecht around 1934, concerning a Gentile woman who was tortured and killed for having had sexual relations with a Jewish man. Both the photograph and the poem have been stenciled on exhibition walls so that the one complements the other. As Rothenberg called attention to Anne Frank's womanliness, so Spero wants the viewer to realize the degree of sexual abuse Nazis visited on women. (Women were undoubtedly sexually abused more than men, but I did know a man who as a young teenager in one of the camps was forced into a male brothel.) Spero has also done wall pieces commemorating the execution of a Jewish partisan, Masha Bruskina, who was captured in the Minsk Ghetto on October 26, 1941 (fig. 38). As other artists have done in their work, in this piece—based on a newspaper photograph of Bruskina's bound body with a noose around her neck, which was displayed at the gates of a factory—Spero provides a name for a victim and reinvests her with a humanity she was denied by her murderers.[44]

Although virtually all the artists have said that implicit in their work is an acknowledgment of and sympathy for victims of other genocides (Armenia, Cambodia, Rwanda, Bosnia), only one artist, as far as I know, has used Holocaust imagery to point up men's victimization of women even if the men themselves have been victimized. At least this would seem to be the position Joan Snyder (born in 1940) takes in her *Women in Camps* (1988) (fig. 39). Juxtaposed are scenes of Jewish and Arab women and children either fleeing or waiting in line. On the right side of the painting are the words "The moon shone in Germany. The moon shines in Palestine and men are still seeking final solutions." She has said: "That is the point of the painting. [It is] about men seeking final solutions, even men who lived through the Holocaust."[45]

Whatever Snyder's attitude, to equate Nazi intentions in the 1940s with Israeli intentions in the 1980s is, on the face of it, morally, politically, and militarily untenable. To recall again Alvin Rosenfeld's admonition:

> To generalize or universalize the victims of the Holocaust is not only to profane their memories, but to exonerate their execution-ers. [For] there are no metaphors for Auschwitz, just as Auschwitz is not a metaphor for anything else. Why is that the case? Because the flames were real flames, the ashes only ashes, the smoke always and only smoke. [The burnings] can only 'be' and 'mean' what they in fact were: the death of the Jews.[46]

No! The connection between Nazis and Jews in the 1940s is not analo-gous to that between Israelis and Arabs decades later—which is not to exonerate Israel's policies in the West Bank, whatever Snyder thinks.

A similar kind of confusion can be found in the attitude Judy Chicago (born in 1939) brought to one of the most ambitious works con-cerned with the Holocaust, her *Holocaust Project,* completed in 1992. From the way in which she explains her understanding of the Holocaust, about which she admits that as late as 1984 she "knew almost nothing," one does not know if she has ever separated the Holocaust itself from other kinds of victimization. For example, she says:

> In exploring the Holocaust, I was learning about the tragic ways Jews had been victimized, and this eventually linked up with my

understanding of women's oppression. I realized that part of
what had led me to the Holocaust was a deep, though previously unarticulated interest in "the victim" experience and that
my previous investigation of the ways women had been treated
historically provided me with an unusual frame of reference for
examining the Jewish experience of the Holocaust. . . . I began
to perceive that the unique experience of the Holocaust could
be a window into an aspect of the unarticulated but universal
human experience of victimization.[47]

My problem with this point of view is not that Chicago came to
the Holocaust through her interest in feminism. Several female artists
have indicated that the social concerns raised by the women's movement
prompted them to think about other public issues, which they realized
were in turn prompted by their Jewish heritage for social justice. Meyer-
Bernstein has said (in 1987) very firmly: "My themes reflect a feminist
point of view dealing with a multitude of female shapes, folds, and concepts. I am linked with pride to my female heritage and express my sol-
idarity with women of the past." And she has also stated that she is
"committed to fight for the elimination of . . . extreme horrors, be they
Hiroshima, Nagasaki, Cambodia, Vietnam, South Africa, Central America, or Bangladesh."[48]

My problem with Chicago is the way one set of atrocities dissolves
into another without qualification, as if they are all equal. A specific
example: Chicago compares a truck driver hauling radioactive waste with
a Polish trainman hauling human cargo to a murder camp: "Tell me: is
the man driving the truck (who is only doing his job) so different from
the trainman in Poland? Doesn't it require the same level of denial and
refusal to confront the consequences of these actions?" If one views every
governmental horror as equal and absolute, there is no difference. But
if one thinks in terms of governmental policies, of reasons for atomic
development, of reasons for the Holocaust, and of genocide, then there
is considerable difference between the truck driver and the trainman.
(I am not arguing here for nuclear diplomacy or even atomic energy
plants, but for separating out the transportation of nuclear waste from
the act of delivering Jews to their certain deaths.)

And while it is conceivable, with the notion only of repression in
mind, to juxtapose, as Chicago does in her "Treblinka/Genocide"

panel, images of Armenians, Hottentots, Australian Aborigines, Gypsies, Native Americans, and Jews (only the Jew is engulfed in flames), or to equate in the "Arbeit Macht Frei" panel images of slavery in the United States with images of slavery in concentration camps, it is not, on the other hand, conceivable to equate the German plan to murder all Jewish people with the repression of the other groups, horrifying as that repression might be.[49]

Art Spiegelman, in telling the story of his parents' experiences during the war, proceeded in the opposite way. In his two "comic novels for adults" (not novels in comic book form), *Maus* and *Maus II*, he insisted on involving himself with small things, actualities, and remembered events, rather than reach for grand political statements. To present his parents' story and their history accurately and effectively, "it soon became clear that I had to engage myself with the specifically Jewish aspects of my parents' situation. Any universalizing could only be achieved through particulars."[50]

It might well be that in the end the most personal is the most gripping, the individual rather than the ideological, the idiosyncratic rather than the general, the specific situation rather than the imposed set of concepts. The popularity of Spiegelman's books does not reside in their curious format but in the thoroughness of the specific story they tell—that of his parents' survival. Listening to survivors reminisce or reading their words in interviews or books is probably still the most moving way to remember and to learn about the Holocaust. Jeffrey A. Wolin (born in 1951) began to interview and photograph survivors in the late 1980s. In the areas around their faces, he prints passages from their interviews (fig. 40). The subjects might mourn their past or celebrate their present, but it is their very words written out for us to read, the look in their eyes, or perhaps something in their posture, that compel complete attention. These are the people who were there. They are the living memory. When the last one dies, we will be terribly diminished.

Wolin explicitly acknowledges this when he says:

> I am fully aware that no one who did not directly experience the Holocaust can truly understand the depths of horror that Jews in Europe experienced at the hands of the Nazis. Nevertheless, it is my hope that by providing a face with an accompanying story of great power, an audience can empathize with the survivors.[51]

Few faces or stories are more powerful, or more moving, than that of Rena Grynblat. She holds a picture of her son, from whom she was separated during the war (a story in itself). She knows that he might have been sent to Treblinka, but then she thinks perhaps not. Perhaps he is still alive. "This way you go with a burden all through your life thinking what happened to him. Maybe he's grown. Maybe he lives next door." (I have been to conferences where people have held a forty- or fifty-year-old photograph of a child and asked if anybody knows this person. I have also seen cousins, separated for that length of time, find each other at such conferences.)

Children raised in Europe also have stories to tell. As French-born American video artist Pier Marton (born in 1951) has said in his twenty-eight-minute video, "Say I Am a Jew" (1985): "Knowing our parents had *almost* been killed many times, we grew up with a particular chill in our bones. The peace treaties had only put a halt to the physical assault: no particular measures had been taken to eradicate anti-Semitism and, in our houses and elsewhere, our families' grief, terror, and anger found very little room to heal." As a result, he and other European children of survivors have fled to the United States to lead lives free of that kind of oppression. But the amount of hatred they absorbed from their environment might never leave them. The fear of having to admit being Jewish was so strong that Marton said he nearly fainted the first time he had to say "I am a Jew" in a group setting.

The video "Say I Am a Jew" records what these Euro-Americans think and feel (fig. 41). Using short sound bites and abrupt cutting, Marton elicited comments that reveal that some people are still deeply scarred, and that no amount of talking will be able to repair their Jewish psyches. Others commented on their newfound strength and pride in their religion. Marton wants Jews and non-Jews to see the video so that people will know how difficult it is to be a Jew and to "see if [he] could get non-Jews to somehow enter the Jewish psyche and see that they are responsible for something in there. Because we are all responsible for one another." After visiting Auschwitz in 1989, Marton began to present the video in a small space that simulated a boxcar. Viewers are then invited to write comments in chalk on the exterior walls.[52]

Although Marton has developed a strong Jewish identity, his "Say I Am a Jew" deals directly with the difficult issues of such identity, particularly for Marton and many of his subjects, who experienced several overt, even physically dangerous anti-Jewish encounters while growing up. By contrast, Jewish Americans born after the war generally have not had encounters of such magnitude or with any frequency. Consequently their use of Holocaust imagery, although not necessarily less emotionally charged, cannot always be as personal. They might weep for the destruction of the East European Jewish culture or exult in its hesitant rebirth in more abstract and elegiac ways, but they cannot always make concrete their images or texts as Marton has done. Their Judaism was not always thrust upon them as it was upon European-born Jews. For some their involvement grew as much from an interest in the religion itself as from a sense of a cultural void, an intentional ignorance of East European life insisted on by their parents. The desire here is not to escape from prejudicial surroundings and then reconstitute a healthier self-image as a Jew in America (as with Marton), or to escape from a provincial background (as in earlier generations), but to reconnect to a culture that could become part of one's identity—to go the other way, so to speak, back to the traditions of one's parents and grandparents.

In this regard Susan Erony might represent many Jewish Americans in her age group, although she speaks only for herself. A child of a Ukrainian-Jewish father, she says that she grew up in a household in which nobody talked about the Holocaust and told few stories about life in the old country. She was not even permitted to study Russian in school. She knew almost nothing of her maternal grandparents. Like so many other children, she was not taught Yiddish or Russian (or Polish, German, Czech, or Hungarian), the language of the adults: "The lack of history left me with a void so many of my and later generations in America feel," she says.

It is not too farfetched an analogy to say, then, that the personal loss of a family history on the individual level parallels the larger loss of Jewish culture brought about by the Holocaust; that interest in that subject, for whatever other reasons, is prompted by being deprived of one's own family history. A principal difference is that one can often discover more about the Holocaust as a whole than about one's family history. Finding out about East European life before the Holocaust is almost like finding out about one's family history. So artists like Erony use Holocaust imagery in part as a surrogate for lost family memory. She says as much in the following observation:

> My current understanding is that the Holocaust is what defined
> me as a Jew; on a personal level, my research fills in the holes
> of my family history. I paint and preserve other people's memo-
> ries as a substitute for my own. I try to understand myself, as a
> Jew in America, born in 1949, and my family, by looking
> through the lens of history of the Jews in Europe.

Of the photographs she has taken of Jewish survivors, and her interactions with them and their offspring, she says these "are the vehicle for transferring memory and for naming. The paintings are the way I mourn and preserve."

Erony is certainly aware of issues larger than her own personal sense of loss. She is well aware of the German attempt to destroy Jewish memory:

> The Holocaust becomes a test case for the issue of remember-
> ing and forgetting. I cannot let the memories alone, not only
> because I am Jewish and mourn my tribe, but also because my
> Jewishness ingrains in me a reverence for memory and a man-
> date to preserve and distribute it.

As a Jew and as an individual with a particular history, she knew by the mid-1980s that she would have to address the Holocaust in her work. By 1990 she began to create works based on photographs of the camps, Jewish cemeteries, and German steelmaking plants. Her *Memorial to the Jews of Lodz #4* (1990) (fig. 42) is about the disintegration and destruction of European Jewish culture not only during the Holocaust but in the decades afterward. In 1989 she found fragments of burned prayerbooks and Bibles outside the sole remaining synagogue in Lodz, Poland, which had burned just two years before. Several books had been printed during the years before World War II. Erony rescued some of the material from being thrown out and made a series of six works from it, but only after gaining approval from rabbinical authorities in deciding not to follow the Jewish tradition of burying such fragments with the appropriate religious obsequies. She felt it "more important to preserve them, to somehow symbolically inter them in works of art, than to bury them."[53] One sees in *Memorial to the Jews of Lodz #4* the ghostlike outline of a head encrusted with pigment, and Hebrew script superimposed on a page of text in the shape of a tombstone, both forms set in an impenetrable landscape of torn fragments of text and pigment. As Erony might put it, the culture is dead, but it is remembered and mourned.

Virtually all Jewish-American artists who use Holocaust imagery have two characteristics in common: Their work is about victims and about the documentary record. Quite literally they act as witnesses to the destruction that was the Holocaust. By accepting the fact that Nazi control was so total, they cannot imagine, or choose not to contemplate, any other way to deal with this subject matter. Rarely can one find examples of Jews attacking their enemies, of the process of rebirth, or of a continuation of Jewish culture. But there are at least two contemporary artists whose works do address the issue of rebirth and resilience: Ellen Levy and Edith Altman.

In a series of works created in 1995, using the Budapest Synagogue as her model, Levy explored the notion of death and resurrection (fig. 43). She was drawn to the location by realizing that, as she watched the building undergoing repair, she could wander in an adjacent courtyard and see many tombstones with terminal dates of 1944 or 1945 on them, the years when the Hungarian Jewish community was being murdered. It is true that the Jewish revival in Hungary has been dramatic, but Levy is quick to observe that the scaffolding in her painting "assumed particular resonance for me, as it seemed to demarcate the long gaps between irretrievable damage and cautious repair."[54] How could it be otherwise? Nevertheless the series is not about mourning and preserving, but about rebuilding and revitalizing, symbolized by the synagogue itself.

Altman's response in *Reclaiming the Symbol/The Act of Memory* (1988–1992) is more personal, more intimate, more direct, and more mystical, all at the same time (fig. 44). She wants nothing less than to reclaim the swastika from the Nazis and restore it to its initial meanings as a symbol of revival and prosperity. As it appears in her multiroom installation, the gold swastika is nine feet tall and is restored to its pre-Nazi configuration. Its color refers to the cabalistic tradition in which gold represents base matter that has been spiritually transformed. On the floor the reflection is that of the black Nazi swastika, its form a mirror image of the original and therefore an impure swastika. In front of it there are six chemical beakers, four of which are filled with powders whose colors mystically neutralize negative energy. The other two beakers contain earth from the Galilee area of Israel, where swastikas have been found on architectural ruins. To the right of the large swastika are panels showing locations where swastikas have been found, and on the left are forty-five paintings of transformed swastikas. On the facing wall there is a chart found at Dachau showing the different colored badges worn by prisoners. Next to it are thirty-two color-coded wooden triangles flanked by a gold star, based on the yellow star worn by Jewish people under the Nazis. The central wall contains texts referring to the way symbols have been used to terrorize people. The number of objects chosen throughout relates to cabalistic mystical numerology.

Altman says that she needed to address the symbols of the six-pointed star she had to wear as a child in Germany and the swastika, which looms in her memory

> as a fear-producing image of my experience—of my people's experience—of victimization. I needed to wrestle with it. . . . My fear [as a child] was so big that I had to make it [the swastika] bigger and bigger and bigger to match the fear until the image was bigger than me so that I could overcome it. I needed to wrestle with it to transform this fear, and go through the dark while never forgetting its lessons.

Acknowledging that the Holocaust is a subject that "may be touched but never grasped," Altman visited her native Germany in 1983 to confirm her feeling that "I was not afraid, and that I was not a victim." She wanted to confront her own memories and those of her father, who had been imprisoned in the 1930s,

> not as a fearful child, [but] as a healthy adult. . . . By taking the swastika apart, by deconstructing its meanings and disempowering it, I hoped to change its fearful energy. In a spiritual and mystical kind of sense, I am exorcising the evil memory of the swastika, in hopes of healing our fear. My art is a healing ritual.[55]

In her response to the swastika, Altman takes a symbol perverted by the Nazis and reclaims it to wipe out the memory of its use by a murderous regime. As such, the installation is as unusual as its concept is interesting. Whether her quest to neutralize the symbol and overcome her fears has been successful is for the future to decide.

Other Issues

Each artist must know that Holocaust imagery is not in great demand. How can such scenes be domesticated to the emotional size of a living room wall? How many potential purchasers are out there for this sort of stuff? Jerome Witkin, when asked why he creates Holocaust scenes, answered, "I have to admit that I don't really know. It's a matter of faith. More and more, I'm doing pictures no one is going to buy" (fig. 26).[56] The issue is unresolvable. An artist who creates "horror-show" works, although honestly felt, might turn away the public. "Mild" images, which might seem too compromising and dishonest, could subvert the horror of the Holocaust. And of course there will always be those who cannot confront any aspect of the Holocaust. I know people who will not see *Schindler's List* or *Shoah* because believe that they will be too disturbed. People have walked out of lectures I have given on Holocaust imagery not out of boredom but because—they told me afterward—the images were too upsetting to contemplate.

Yet the artists obviously persist. Marlene E. Miller has said that her sculpture

> *is not* the Holocaust; it is my intention however to make my work come as close to confronting the viewer with the horror as possible without forcing them to turn away. . . . The content might repel, but viewers, although not liking what they see, are compelled to examine their feelings about the content.
> Although they might be uncomfortable, they also feel the safety of knowing that this isn't the 'real thing.'

Her comments refer not only to her *Schlafwagen: Who Will Say Kaddish for Them?* (fig. 33), but to her series of works entitled *Zachor: Remember,* completed in 1996. Each work is presented as a tableau composed of skeletal figures made from papier-mâché. In one, under the notorious sign ARBEIT MACHT FREI, three figures are caught in a maze of barbed wire, the central one posed as in a crucifixion. In another, entitled "Kristallnacht: Die Metzgerei [the butcher shop]," three skeletal figures are shown hanging, two by the neck, one by the wrists. Around the figures are fragments of photographs and bits and pieces of objects. These works do not confront the viewer with the dead and the near dead as if in a Halloween production, but in a Holocaust presentation.

Her art, then, is put to the service of something or something else—asking, remembering, witnessing, not necessarily creating salable works. For, Miller says:

> This safety [of knowing this is not the real thing] enables them to ask the first and most logical question, "Why did this happen?" which cannot be answered until the second query is formed, "How could this happen?" The first question holds no rational answers; the second holds the key to understanding the unfathomableness of the first; it holds the key to learning about the Holocaust which in turn can lead to change.[57]

In so many words, Miller creates these works for the sake of *tikkun olam*, the repair of the world, and this desire, as with so many other artists, is a more formidable motivating agent than catering to the tastes of potential clients. Witkin concurs as well. After visiting Auschwitz in 1990, he concluded that, whatever else he might feel about the murder camp and its purposes, "Now crowds visit to learn how to be better human beings and to pay homage at the biggest cemetery in the world"[58] But it is not just *tikkun olam*. Artists seem to feel: The Holocaust occurred. People are forgetting. People are denying. We can't let that happen and still be self-respecting Jews.

In his own way Natan Nuchi addresses this and related issues and dilemmas in a statement he prepared in 1994, from which I would like to quote at some length:

> The large-scale image of the single, naked, bald, and emaciated figure [fig. 31], particularly the white-skinned powerless male, goes against consumeristic and capitalistic ideals of optimism, activism, and the attainment of power. In this context, my art points also to our culture's difficulty with the Holocaust and the constant need it has to subvert and reshape the Holocaust's meaning to fit its own ideals. Mortality, vulnerability, and being victimized are either repressed or kept in low profile, and can be generally tolerated in the art of this society, only if the aesthetic pleasure, such as metaphor, beauty, form, richness of texture and material, etc., can surpass the harshness and pain of the subject matter. Regardless of quality, most of the art that becomes acceptable to our society, and ultimately is shown in our museums, has much to do with what initially the patrons of

art find suitable to hang on their living room walls. It seems to
me that for art to be congenial to living room surroundings and
be in any meaningful way reflective of the horror and extreme
experience of the Holocaust is an impossibility, a failure, or a
contradiction that might ultimately cause us to change either
our perception of the Holocaust or our expectations from art.

On the other hand, it might also mean learning to think about art as a
conveyor of visual information rather than only as an aesthetic enter-
prise. I doubt if this will ever happen, so the dilemma will remain. At
the least, Holocaust imagery will be honored, but it will never become
popular without serious compromises.

Nuchi's observations bring us to the question of aestheticizing the
Holocaust. At one extreme author Michael Wyschograd floated the
idea that art is not appropriate to the Holocaust because it takes the sting
out of suffering. "It transforms suffering into a catharsis for which
people are willing to pay money to experience." The Holocaust, in this
context, must remain as life and not be transformed into art. "It is
therefore forbidden," he asserts, "to make fiction of the Holocaust."[59]
It is not known if Wyschograd knew Theodor Adorno's famous apho-
rism: "To write poetry after Auschwitz is barbaric," or if he was aware
of Adorno's retraction some years later: "Perennial suffering has as
much right to expression as a tortured man has to scream; hence it
may have been wrong to say that after Auschwitz you could no longer
write poems."[60] Others have written about the morality of writing or
not writing and, by extension, painting or not painting about the Holocaust. For me this is a nonissue and their thoughts are irrelevant, since
I do not accept anybody's parameters on how to approach the Holocaust
or how to contemplate it. In Billie Holiday's famous phrase: "Ain't
nobody's business what I do." And the same holds for the artists. They
remember, memorialize, witness as they can and because they want to.
One may judge the quality and intention of the work produced and find
it in varying degrees aesthetically acceptable or politically exploitive, but
that is quite different from inventing limits or proscriptions.

Murray Zimiles, when confronted with the perplexing question of
how to convey the horror of the Holocaust without distancing the subject by aestheticizing it, answered that in effect there was no question
(fig. 9):

> [My] art was born from necessity, a necessity to tell my story,
> and the story of my people, to purge my demons. . . . Yes, I
> would "aestheticize" the Holocaust if that's what it took to tell
> the story, a story that is being forgotten and is even unknown to
> many of my students. I would use the slashing of the brush, the
> texturing of the palette knife, the blackness of the ink, the red-
> ness of the Nazi flag and of the blood of the victims. . . . To
> deny the necessity for me to do this would be to "aestheticize"
> my soul.

And probably anesthetize it, as well. Then Zimiles asked rhetorically—
how could he not deal with the Holocaust?[61]

Wendy Joy Kuppermann faces the same set of issues from a
slightly different point of view. For her the Holocaust is not just about
its victims and survivors, but about her own connection to it and her sense
of art and craft (fig. 17). Her works are about the Holocaust, about her
own presence in her works, and about quality. For Kuppermann it is a
given that the Holocaust is evil, the very embodiment of evil. Art for her
is good; it is a gift: "I believe that Art at its best provides an imperative
moral function to educate, enlighten, challenge, invigorate, and bind all
manner of peoples and cultures," she has said. And so presumably the
better the art is, the more the evil of the Holocaust can be challenged.

To that end she admits to have done "something questionable back
in my darkroom: I made some beautiful pictures of horrible things, and
I did it on purpose," by teasing out patterns of wood grains and hard
lights on metal surfaces. She has manipulated shadows and addressed
formal problems of balance and symmetry, all the while knowing that
she was creating works "in the ruins of human suffering and chaos."
Of her images of train tracks, barracks, shower heads, and fences, she
has felt that she needed "to own them personally as I inhabit them daily.
. . . I put myself in the picture." Such gestures of empathy derive from
her experiences as a child of survivors, which she considers to be timeless. She reaches back to images of places of the past, her parents'
past, and reinterprets them for the present so that she can possess
them as if she had been there. As deeply a part of her being as they are
for the survivors.[62]

The profoundly serious tone of Kuppermann's observations and
commitments, like those of the other artists, clearly suggests that the issue

is not: Should one aestheticize or should one not aestheticize? It is not an either-or proposition, but rather one in which concerns of composition, line, shape, and color become the means by which the subject is presented and that allow it to carry a necessary conviction and—of equal importance—the compelling psychological weight artists have invested in it. From this point of view, strictly formal analyses or descriptions of such works are insulting.

Nor does the subject matter lend itself to current postmodern sensibilities. Perhaps one might say instead that the use of Holocaust imagery is a way to avoid such sensibilities. For if we assume that postmodernism is characterized by a sense of irony, a willingness to deny authorial responsibility through open-ended formulations, a desire to manipulate means and materials to suggest levels of unfixity in regard to content and form, then most works by these artists are decidedly not postmodern. Ellen Rothenberg's *The Anne Frank Project* is a notable exception because of the multivalent responses it is intended to provoke (fig. 37). One might wish to argue that this work is among the most stylistically and conceptually advanced works using Holocaust imagery, quite different from the more traditionally responsive works of the other artists, but its meanings are in no way totally open-ended. It is about Anne Frank—her life, her times, and her possibilities. It is not morally ambiguous or neutral; neither is it just about process and viewer response to process. Postmodern techniques and devices of presentation are present, but the purposes of the work are focused.

Nuchi related an anecdote about browsing in a bookstore that may help to explain why so many other Jewish-American artists turned to Holocaust themes in the late 1970s and 1980s:

> It was quite a sobering experience, standing in the bookstore, browsing through art magazines, looking at works by contemporary American artists, and then moving on to the Judaica section to look at pictures from the Holocaust. The artists' preoccupation with the "non-authentic" and all-knowing irony forever hovering over the works, the Jasper Johnsian chess games and iconographic crossword puzzles, the quotations and recyclings of images from the history of art and their fusion with popular and pornographic images, as well as all this cultural rumination, as sophisticated as it was, seemed to me like

some mental fatigue. But as far as the photographs that came
to us from the Holocaust are concerned, I believe they are
among the very few images in our culture which cannot be
treated with irony. In the mid-80s, it seemed that there wasn't
an image high or low that was not fair game for recycling,
appropriation, or simulation and for arbitrary coupling with
other images.[63]

Assuming that other artists went through a similar thought process, finding a viable subject matter able to bear the weight of personal statement,
heartfelt commitment, moral argument, clear authorial voice, community engagement, and communicability became important, even imperative. Given the ways in which Jewish-American artists had begun to
think about themselves, their connections to Judaism, their thoughts about
the dying out of the survivors, and the general situation of Jewish
people in the country in the 1970s, it becomes easier to understand
why so many turned to Holocaust imagery. They had come to better terms
with the sense of their own Jewishness at the same time that they
rejected various aspects of postmodernism.

Most would probably agree with Pier Marton, who said: "As a non-
religious Jew, you have only a tradition of martyrdom. I don't say that
one needs to become religious. But to look at this huge body of Jewish
knowledge and not do your best to pass it on, to honor it, is another type
of murder."[64] In their different ways these artists are honoring and
passing on that body of knowledge—both as a means of self-identification
as Jews and as a way to identify with other Jews, and in the hope that
their images will become part of the heritage that is passed on to future
generations.

NOTES

Preface

1. Ziva Amishai-Maisels, *Depiction and Interpretation: The Influence of the Holocaust on the Visual Arts* (New York: Pergamon Press, 1993), 1–567.
2. Monica Bohm-Duchen, ed., *After Auschwitz: Responses to the Holocaust in Contemporary Art* (Sunderland, England: Northern Centre for Contemporary Art in association with Lund Humphries Publishers Limited, 1995), 1–160.

Prologue: Children of Survivors—"Memorial Candles"

1. Statement in "Never Again," curated by Noga Garrison, Cathedral of St. John the Divine, New York, 1995, n.p.; letter to author, Oct. 14, 1995.
2. Arthur A. Cohen, *The Tremendum: A Theological Interpretation of the Holocaust* (New York: Crossroad Publishing Co., 1981), 2, cited in Alan L. Berger, *Crisis and Covenant: The Holocaust in American Jewish Fiction* (Albany: SUNY Press, 1985), 11.
3. Wendy Joy Kuppermann, "The Far Country: A Photographic Journey," typescript, 1994.
4. Dina Waldi, *Memorial Candles: Children of the Holocaust,* trans. Naomi Goldblum (London: Tavistock/Routledge, 1992), 6, 32.
5. Vivian Alpert Thompson, *A Mission in Art* (Macon, Ga.: Macon University Press, 1988), 94; letter to author, May 30, 1995.
6. Lawrence Langer, *Admitting the Holocaust: Collected Essays* (New York: Oxford University Press, 1995), 18.

7. Kuppermann, "The Far Country: A Photographic Journey"; Wendy Joy Kuppermann, "Installation: 'The Far Country': Artist's Statement," typescript, 1995.

8. Letter to author, Apr. 13, 1996.

9. Elyse Klaidman, "Elyse Klaidman/Painting," typescript, n.d.

10. Paul Kresh, "Photograph Exhibit Evokes Memories of Holocaust," *Jewish Weeks, Inc.* (May 10–16, 1991): 38, cited in Stephen C. Feinstein, "Witness and Legacy," *Witness and Legacy: Contemporary Art about the Holocaust* (St. Paul, Minn.: Museum of American Art, 1995), 17; *St. Paul Pioneer Press,* sec. E, Jan. 29, 1995, 1.

11. Statement accompanying exhibition, *Say I Am a Jew,* May 1990; letter to author, Nov. 12, 1995.

12. Letter to author, Nov. 21, 1995.

13. For Salamon see Alexander Wohl, "Interview with Julie Salamon," *Baltimore Jewish Times,* Feb. 19, 1998, 60, cited in Alan L. Berger, "Ashes and Hope: The Holocaust in Second Generation American Literature," in Randolph L. Brahan, ed., *Reflections of the Holocaust in Art and Literature* (Boulder, Colo.: Social Science Monographs, 1990), 104. For the second citation, see Lucy Y. Steinitz with David M. Szony, eds., *After the Holocaust: Reflections by Children of Survivors in America,* rev. 2d ed. (New York: Bloch, 1979), ii.

Before the War

1. Diego Rivera, *Portrait of America* (New York: Covici Friede, 1934), 21–32. See also *The Nation* 137 (Sept. 6, 1933): 257–258; and *Art Digest* 7 (Aug. 1, 1933): 12.

2. Deborah E. Lipstadt, *Beyond Belief: The American Press and the Coming of the Holocaust, 1933–1945* (New York: Free Press, 1986), 36.

3. Susan Noyes Platt, "The Jersey Homesteads Mural: Ben Shahn, Bernarda Bryson and History Painting in the 1930s," in Patricia M. Burnham and Lucretia Hoover Giese, eds., *Redefining American History Painting* (New York: Cambridge University Press, 1995), 302.

4. Frances K. Pohl, "Constructing History: A Mural by Ben Shahn," *Arts Magazine* 62 (Sept. 1987): 38–39; and Amishai-Maisels, *Depiction and Interpretation:* 374.

5. Max Weber, "The Reminiscences of Max Weber," vol. 1, Oral History Research Office, Columbia University, New York, 1958, p. 29. I want to thank Marsha Kunin for calling this citation to my attention.

6. Dorothy Seidman Bilik, in her *Immigrant Survivors: Post-Holocaust Consciousness in Recent Jewish American Fiction* (Middletown, Conn.: Wesleyan University Press, 1981), 77, makes a similar point concerning Bernard Malamud's writings, decades later, about immigrants and refugees.

7. Lucy Dawidowicz, *The War Against the Jews: 1933–1945* (New York: Bantam, 1976), 106. See also chronologies of persecution listed in Lucy Dawidowicz, *A Holocaust Reader* (West Orange, N.J.: Behrman House, 1976), 35–55; and Carol Rittner and John Roth, eds., *Different Voices: Women and the Holocaust* (New York: Paragon House, 1993), 22–32.

8. Amishai-Maisels, *Depiction and Interpretation*, 374.

9. *Art Digest* 7 (Mar. 15, 1933): 7; 7 (Nov. 1, 1933): 7; 8 (Aug. 1, 1934): 9; 8 (Sept. 1, 1934): 13; 10 (Oct. 1, 1935): 3; 11 (Nov. 15, 1936): 9; 11 (Dec. 15, 1936): editorial page; 11 (Aug. 1, 1937): 17. See also *Art Front* 2 (Jan. 1937): 3; *Magazine of Art* 30 (Jan. 1937): 65; and 30 (Aug. 1937): 496–497.

10. Lipstadt, *Beyond Belief*, 9 and passim.

11. Ilan Avisar, *Screening the Holocaust: Cinema's Images of the Unimaginable* (Bloomington: Indiana University Press, 1988), 92, 96.

12. See, for example, ibid., 99; Lipstadt, *Beyond Belief*, 47; Leonard Dinnerstein, *America and the Survivors of the Holocaust* (New York: Columbia University Press, 1982), 1, 6; and Haskell Lookstein, *Were We Our Brother's Keepers?: The Public Response of American Jews to the Holocaust, 1938–1944* (New York: Hartmore House, 1985), 31.

13. Thomas Craven, *Modern Art: The Men, the Movements, the Meaning* (New York: Simon & Schuster, 1934), 312.

14. Matthew Baigell, "Benton and the Left," in R. Douglas Hurt and Mary K. Davis, eds., *Thomas Hart Benton: Artist, Writer, and Intellectual* (Jefferson City: State Historical Society of Missouri, 1989), 19–23.

15. Moses Soyer, "The Second Whitney Biennial," *Art Front* 1 (Feb. 1935): 7–8.

16. Arthur Liebman, "Anti-Semitism on the Left?" in David A. Gerber, ed., *Anti-Semitism in American History* (Urbana: University of Illinois Press, 1987), 342.

17. Bat-Ami Zucher, "American Jewish Communists and Jewish Culture in the 1930s," *Modern Judaism* 14 (1994): 175–178; and Matthew Baigell, "From Hester Street to Fifty-seventh Street: Jewish-American Artists in New York," in Norman L. Kleeblatt and Susan Chevlowe, eds., *Painting a Place in America: Jewish Artists in New York, 1900–1945* (New York: Jewish Museum, 1991), 50–62.

18. For Browder, see Earl Browder, *Communism in the United States* (New York: International Publishers, 1935), cited in Loren Baritz, ed., *The American Left: Radical Political Thought in the Twentieth Century* (New York: Basic Books, 1971), 252. For Wolfe, see "What Will I Do When America Goes to War? A Symposium," *Modern Monthly* 9 (Sept. 1935), cited in ibid., 306.

19. Louis Ruchanes, "Jewish Radicalism in the United States," in Peter I. Rose, ed., *The Ghetto and Beyond* (New York: Random House, 1969), 246–247; World Alliance of Yiddish Culture, "YKUF," Art Section USA, *First Exhibition* (New York: 1938), n.p.; Harvey Klehr, *The Heyday of American Communism: The Depression Decade* (New York: Basic Books, 1984), 383; Zucher, "American Jewish Communists," 180–181; Norman L. Kleeblatt and Susan Chevlowe, "Painting a Place in America," in their *Painting a Place in America*, 135–142.

20. Amishai-Maisels, *Depiction and Representation*, 78.

The War

1. Lipstadt, *Beyond Belief*, 38–39, 127, 252–254.

2. James E. Young, *The Texture of Memory: Holocaust Memorials and Meaning* (New Haven, Conn.: Yale University Press, 1993), 287–288.

3. Lipstadt, *Beyond Belief,* 254

4. Bilik, *Immigrant Survivors,* 29; Edward Alexander, "The Holocaust in American-Jewish Fiction: A Slow Awakening," in Jacob Neusner, ed., *In the Aftermath of the Holocaust* (New York: Garland, 1993), 3; William B. Helmreich, "The Impact of Holocaust Survivors on American Society: A Socio-Cultural Portrait," *Judaism* 39 (Winter 1990): 14–15; Stephen J. Whitfield, "The Holocaust and the American Jewish Intellectual," in Neusner, *In the Aftermath,* 241–245; Irving Howe, *A Margin of Hope* (New York: Harcourt Brace Jovanovich, 1982), 248–250; Shoshona Felman and Dori Laub, *Testimony: Crises of Witnessing in Literature, Psychoanalysis, and History* (New York: Routledge, 1992), 81, 191–192; and Terry A. Cooney, *The Rise of the New York Intellectuals: Partisan Review and Its Circle* (Madison: University of Wisconsin Press, 1986), 229–250.

5. Primo Levi, *The Drowned and the Saved,* trans. Raymond Rosenthal (New York: Summit Books, 1986), 21; Zygmunt Bauman, *Modernity and the Holocaust* (Ithaca, N.Y.: Cornell University Press, 1991), 32; Rittner and Roth, *Different Voices,* 1, 189; and James E. Young, *Writing and Rewriting the Holocaust: Narrative and the Consequences of Interpretation* (Bloomington: Indiana University Press, 1990), 189.

6. Sander Gilman, *Jewish Self-Hatred: Anti-Semitism and the Hidden Language of the Jews* (Baltimore: Johns Hopkins University Press, 1986), 305; Raphael Patai, *The Jewish Mind* (New York: Charles Scribner's Sons, 1977), 461–462; and Estelle Frankel, "The Promise and Pitfalls of Jewish Relationships," *Tikkun* 5 (Sept. 1990): 19, 95.

7. For a much less schematized reading of the postwar situation, see Alexander, "The Holocaust in America-Jewish Fiction," 5–6; Judith Miller, *One, by One, by One, Facing the Holocaust* (New York: Simon & Schuster, 1990), 220–221; Edward Shapiro, *A Time for Healing: American Jewry Since World War II* (Baltimore: Johns Hopkins University Press, 1992), 3–8, 24–25, 61, 213; and David A. Teutch, ed., *Imagining the Jewish Future: Essays and Responses* (Albany: State University Press of New York, 1992), 3.

8. My discussion of Greenberg's comments in "Under Forty: A Symposium on American Literature and the Younger Generation of American Jews," in *Contemporary Jewish Record* (1944) is taken from Cooney, *The Rise of the New York Intellectuals,* 237–239.

9. Clement Greenberg, "Self-Hatred and Jewish Chauvinism," *Commentary* 10 (Nov. 1950): 426–433.

10. Harold Rosenberg, "Is There a Jewish Art?" *Commentary* 42 (July 1966): 59. See also "Jews in Art" (1975) in Harold Rosenberg, *Art and Other Serious Matters* (Chicago: University of Chicago Press, 1985), 58–69.

11. Emery Grossman, *Art and Tradition* (New York: Thomas Yoseloff, 1967), 47; and James Fitzsimmons, "Artists Put Faith in New Ecclesiastic Art," *Art Digest* 26 (Oct. 15, 1951): 23. See also Norman L. Kleeblatt and Vivian B. Mann, eds., *Treasures of the Jewish Museum* (New York: Universe Books, 1986), 190.

12. Grossman, *Art and Tradition,* 96.

13. Stephen Robert Frankel, ed., *Jack Levine* (New York: Rizzoli, 1989), 37, 55.

14. Irma B. Jaffe, *The Sculpture of Leonard Baskin* (New York: Viking Press, 1980), 127.

15. Conversation with author in artist's studio, Feb. 3, 1994.

16. Illustrated in *Art Digest* 17 (Jan. 15, 1943): 16

17. Cecile Whiting, *Antifascism in American Art* (New Haven, Conn.: Yale University Press, 1989), 165.

18. Albert Elsen, *Seymour Lipton* (New York: Harry N. Abrams, 1974), 27–28; Seymour Lipton, "Some Notes on My Sculpture," *Magazine of Art* 40 (Oct. 1947): 264; "Harris Rosenstein, "Lipton's Code," *Art News* 76 (Mar. 1971): 47; Elsen, *Lipton,* 27.

19. For the complete text see John W. McCoubrey, ed., *American Art, 1700–1960: Sources and Documents* (Englewood Cliffs, N.J.: Prentice-Hall, 1965), 210–212.

20. Friedrich Nietzsche, *The Birth of Tragedy and The Case of Wagner,* trans. Walter Kaufman (New York: Vintage Books, 1967), 60.

21. Anna C. Chave, *Mark Rothko: Subjects in Abstraction* (New Haven, Conn.: Yale University Press, 1989), 88–89, 85. See also James E. B. Breslin, *Mark Rothko: A Biography* (Chicago: University of Chicago, 1993), 166.

22. The transcript of the radio broadcast, which took place on October 13, 1943, is in Laurence Alloway and Mary Davis MacNaughton, *Adolph Gottlieb: A Retrospective* (New York: The Arts Publisher, Inc., 1981), 170–171.

23. Chave, *Mark Rothko,* 89.

24. Matthew Baigell, "Barnett Newman's Stripe Paintings and Kabbalah: A Jewish Take," *American Art* 8 (Spring 1994): 33–43. See also Gershom Scholem, *Major Trends in Jewish Mysticism* (1946; reprint, New York: Schocken, 1961), 260–276; and Thomas Hess, *Barnett Newman* (New York: Museum of Modern Art, 1971), 56, 71, 52–61, and 83.

25. Barnett Newman, "The Sublime Is Now" (1948), in John O'Neill, ed., *Barnett Newman: Selected Writings and Interviews* (Berkeley: University of California Press, 1990), 170.

26. Mira Goldfarb, "Sacred Signs and Symbols in Morris Louis: The Charred Journal Series, 1951" (Master's Thesis, City College of the City University of New York, 1993), 58, 54. I thank the author for allowing me to read her thesis.

27. Amishai-Maisels, *Depiction and Interpretation,* 28–29, 198–202, 21–23, and 174–177.

28. Sidney J. Freedberg, "Bloom: Macabre Anatomy," *Art News* 47 (Feb. 1949): 52; Amashai-Maisels, *Depiction and Interpretation,* 82; Selden Rodman, *The Eye of Man: Form and Content in Western Painting* (New York: Devin-Adair, 1955), 157.

29. Frankel, ed., *Jack Levine,* 134; and Amishai-Maisels, *Depiction and Interpretation,* 83.

30. Raphael Soyer, *Self-Revealment: A Memoir* (New York: Random House, 1967), 110.

31. William Gropper, *Your Brother's Blood Cries Out* (New York: New Masses, 1943).

32. August L. Freundlich, *William Gropper: Retrosepctive* (Miami, Fla.: University of Miami Joe and Emily Lowe Art Gellery, 1968), 29, 28.

33. Ben Shahn, *The Shape of Content* (New York: Vintage Books, 1957), 55.

34. Amishai-Maisels, *Depiction and Interpretation,* 310–311. See also her "Ben Shahn and the Problem of Jewish Identity," *Jewish Art* 12–13 (1986–1987): 304.

35. Ben-Zion, "An Artist's View of a Jewish Museum," *Jewish News* (Sept. 13, 1963): 53, microfilm, Archives of American Art, roll N69-122, frame 153.

36. From the catalog statement, Archives of American Art, roll N69-122, frame 265; see also frame 194; Alfred Werner, "Ben-Zion, Jewish Painter," *Midstream* 19 (Nov. 1973): 33–34; and "In Memoriam," *Art Digest* 21 (Dec. 15, 1946): 15.

37. David G. Roskies, *Against the Apocalypse: Responses to Catastrophe in Modern Jewish Culture* (Cambridge, Mass.: Harvard University Press, 1984), 13, 16. See also Saul Friedländer, "Trauma, Memory and Transference," in Geoffrey H. Hartman, ed., *Holocaust Remembrance: The Shape of Memory* (Cambridge, England: Blackwell, 1994), 255.

38. Emil Fackenheim, *To Mend the World: Foundations of Post-Holocaust Thought* (New York: Schocken Books, 1982), 193–194.

39. Yosef Hayim Yerushalmi, *Zakhor* (Seattle: University of Washington Press, 1982), 22.

40. For further discussion of this point, see Geoffrey H. Hartman, "Public Memory and Its Discontents," *Raritan* 13 (Spring 1994): 30.

41. Langer, *Admitting the Holocaust,* 25–26.

42. Emil Fackenheim, "Reflections on Aliyah," *Midstream* 3 (Aug.–Sept. 1985): 25–26, cited in Avisar, *Screening the Holocaust,* 50.

43. Lawrence Langer, *Holocaust Testimonies: The Ruins of Memory* (New Haven, Conn.: Yale University Press, 1991), 160–161.

Postwar Responses

1. S. Lillian Kremer, *Witness Through the Imagination: Jewish American Holocaust Literature* (Detroit: Wayne State University Press, 1989), 357. See also Peter Novick, "Holocaust Memory in America," in James E. Young, ed., *The Art of Memory: Holocaust Memorials in History* (New York: Jewish Museum, 1994), 159–162; and Miller, *One, by One, by One,* 220–228.

2. Teutch, ed., *Imagining the Jewish Future,* 3; and Michael Berenbaum, "The Nativization of the Holocaust," *Judaism* 35 (Fall 1986): 447.

3. Shapiro, *A Time for Healing,* 213; and Miller, *One, by One, by One,* 223. See also Jacob Neusner, *Stranger at Home: "The Holocaust," Zionism, and American Judaism* (Chicago: University of Chicago Press, 1981), 68, 78.

4. Langer, *Admitting the Holocaust,* 52; Levi, *The Drowned and the Saved,* 24; George Steiner, *Language and Silence* (New York: Atheneum, 1966), 143–144, cited in Bilik, *Immigrant Survivors,* 42; Leonard Fein, *Where Are We? The Inner Life of American Jews* (New York: Harper & Row, 1988), 60, cited in Shapiro, *A Time for Healing,* 213; Donald Kuspit, "The Abandoned Nude: Natan Nuchi's Paintings," in Kuspit, *Natan Nuchi* (New York: Klarfeld Perry Gallery, 1992), n.p.; and Alfred Kazin, *New York Jew* (New York: Vintage, 1979), 39.

5. Jack Levin and Jack McDermott, *Hate Crimes: The Rising Tide of Bigotry and Bloodshed* (New York: Plenum Press, 1993), 40.

6. Daniel Jeremy Silver, "Choose Life," *Judaism* 35 (Fall 1986): 446; Jonathan Boyarin, *Storm from Paradise: The Politics of Jewish Memory* (Minneapolis: University of Minnesota Press, 1992): xiii; and Sara Bershtel and Allen Graubard, *Saving Remnants: Feeling Jewish in America* (New York: Free Press, 1992), 119.

7. Anne Roiphe, *Generation Without Memory: A Jewish Journey in Christian America* (New York: Summit Books, 1981), 176; Norma Rosen, "The Second Life of Holocaust Imagery," *Midstream* 33 (Apr. 1987): 59; and Annette Wieviorka, "On Testimony" in Hartman, ed., *Holocaust Remembrance*, 24.

8. Belle Krasne, "Ten Artists on the Margin," *Design Quarterly* 30 (Spring 1954): 22, cited in Peter Selz, *Harold Persico Paris, 1925–1979* (San Francisco: Harcourts Modern and Contemporary Art, 1992), n.p.

9. Selz, *Harold Persico Paris;* and Peter Selz, "The Final Negation: Harold Paris' Koddesh Koddashim," *Art in America* 57 (Mar./Apr. 1969): 62, 66.

10. Selz, *Harold Persico Paris;* and Bruce Nixon, "In an Atmosphere of Mourning: Harold Paris at Judah L. Magnes Museum," *Artweek* 25 (Nov. 17, 1994): 12.

11. Gerald Marzorati, *A Painter of Darkness: Leon Golub and Our Times* (New York: Penguin Books, 1990), 166.

12. Ibid., 165, 164; Donald Kuspit, *Leon Golub: Existential/Activist Painter* (New Brunswick, N.J.: Rutgers University Press, 1985), 38, 39; Peter Selz, *New Images of Man* (New York: Museum of Modern Art, 1959), 76; and Irving Sandler, "Rhetoric and Violence: Interview with Leon Golub," *Arts Magazine* 44 (Feb. 1970): 23.

13. Alvin Rosenfeld, *A Double Dying: Reflections on Holocaust Literature* (Bloomington: Indiana University Press, 1980), 160; and Avisar, *Screening the Holocaust*, 91.

14. For Klement see Vera Klement file, Jewish Museum; for Fishman, see *Jewish Themes/Contemporary American Artists II* (New York: Jewish Museum, 1986), 12; for the others see *Jewish Themes: Northern California Artists* (Berkeley, Calif.: Judah L. Magnes Museum, 1987), 13, 14, 16.

15. Kuppermann, "Installation: 'The Far Country': Artist's Statement," 1995.

16. Letter from Archi Rand to author, Apr. 13, 1992.

17. Vladimir Jankelevitch, "Should We Pardon Them?" trans. Ann Hobart, *Critical Inquiry* 22 (Spring 1996): 564. From *Pardonner?* (Paris, 1971). For Galles, see letter to author, Apr. 11, 1996.

Tikkun Olam

1. For Zimiles see *The Holocaust in Contemporary Art* (Trenton, N.J.: Trenton State College, 1989), n.p.; and *Murray Zimiles: The Holocaust Series, 1986–1993* (Madeira Beach, Fla.: Holocaust Memorial Museum and Educational Center, 1994), n.p. For Chafetz see letter to author, Dec. 12, 1995.

2. Letter from Gerda Meyer-Bernstein to author, Mar. 3, 1994.

3. For Oransky see letter to author, Mar. 3, 1994. For Witkin, see letters to author, Dec. 12, 1992 and Mar. 25, 1994. See also Sherry Chayat, *Life Lessons: The Art of Jerome Witkin* (Syracuse, N.Y.: Syracuse University Press, 1994), p. 28.

4. Ora Lerman, "Autobiographical Journey: Can Art Transform Personal and

Cultural Loss?" *Arts Magazine* 59 (May 1985): 103; and Mac Mcloud, "History as Renewal," in *Ruth Weisberg Prints: Mid-Life Catalogue Raisonné, 1961–1990* (Fresno, Calif.: Fresno Art Museum, 1990), 23.

5. Borenstein's poem was printed in Charles Fishman, ed., *Blood to Remember: American Poets on the Holocaust* (Lubbock: Texas Tech University Press, 1991), 8. It is a Jewish custom to leave a pebble on the tombstone when visiting a gravesite. The shofar, a ram's horn, is sounded on the High Holy Days. For Salamon see Berger, "Ashes and Hope: The Holocaust in Second Generation American Literature," 107. For Levine see Meg Levine, *The Boulder Holocaust Remembrance Project Archive* (© Meg Levine, 1994), n.p., and letter to author July 13, 1994.

6. For Beerman see Gert Schiff, *Primal Ground: Miriam Beerman: Works from 1983–1987* (Montclair, N.J.: Montclair Art Museum, 1988), cited in *The Holocaust in Contemporary Art*, n.p.; For Brand see Bohm-Duchen, *After Auschwitz*, 148; for Cahana, telephone conversation with author, Apr. 19, 1994.

7. Scholem, *Major Trends in Jewish Mysticism*, 268.

8. For Weisberg, see letter to author, Apr. 2, 1994. For Cohen, see statement, "Never Again."

9. For Stein, "Never Again."

10. David McCracken, "Spertus Exhibit a Different Look at Traditions," *Chicago Tribune*, May 6, 1988, sec. 7, p. 47; Sue Taylor, "Memory Is Woven into Altman's Work," *Chicago Sun Times*, May 7, 1987 (clipping); Christopher English, *Edith Altman* (Chicago: N.A.M.E. Gallery, 1987), n.p.; Mary Jane Jacob, "The Artist in Society," *Kunstarbeit* (Chicago: State of Illinois Art Gallery, 1992), 4; Joseph S. Mella, *Edith Altman: Photography, Text, Object* (Rockford, Ill.: Rockford Art Museum, 1989), n.p.; and Gilbert Jimenez, "Altman Tries to Provoke Thought," *Chicago Sun Times*, May 6, 1988, p. 27.

11. *And There Was a Train Full of Children: Pastel Drawings and Constructions* (Pittsburgh: Holocaust Center of the United Jewish Federation and the University of Pittsburgh, 1991), n.p.; *And There Was a Train Full of Children* (Fort Meyers, Fla.: The William R. Frizzell Cultural Center, 1993), n.p.; "Never Again."

12. For Hirshfield, see letter to author, May 5, 1992. For Kalb, see letter to author, March 18, 1994.

13. For Baron, statement in [Los Angeles] *Reader* 10 (Nov. 20, 1987), concerning an exhibition at Jack Rutberg, Fine Arts, Inc., See also file at the Jewish Museum; and Peter Frank, *Hannelore Baron: Collages and Box Constructions* (New York and Los Angeles: Barbara Mathes Gallery and Manny Silverman Gallery, n.d.), 7. For Cahana, see Barbara Rose, *From Ashes to the Rainbow: The Art of Alice Lok Cahana* (Los Angeles: Hebrew Union College Skirball Museum, 1986), 34, 39.

14. For Galles see letter to author, Apr. 11, 1996. For Lerner, see Michael Lerner, *Jewish Renewal: A Path to Healing and Transformation* (New York: HarperCollins, 1994), 203.

15. *Gates of Repentance: The New Union Prayerbook for the Days of Awe* (New York: Central Conference of American Rabbis, 1978), 25; and Jankelevitch, "Should We Pardon Them?" 572.

On Biblical and Mythological Imagery

1. Matthew Baigell, "Segal's 'Holocaust Memorial': An Interview with George Segal," *Art in America* 71 (Summer 1983): 134, 136, reprinted in Young, *The Art of Memory*, 83–87; Doug Adams, "George Segal's 'The Holocaust': Biblical Subject Matter and God as Center," *Transcendence with the Human Body in Art* (New York: Crossroad, 1991), 14–34; Stephen Lewis, *Art Out of Agony: The Holocaust Theme in Literature, Sculpture, and Film* (Toronto: CBC Enterprises, 1984), 111–114; Sam Hunter and Don Hathaway, *George Segal* (New York: Rizzoli, 1984), 132–134; Amishai-Maisels, *Depiction and Interpretation*, 88–90.
2. Statement, *The Artworks of Tibor Spitz* (Rockland, N.Y.: Rockland Center for Holocaust Studies, 1993), n.p.; and letter to author, February 10, 1996.
3. Letter from Pier Marton to author, Apr. 14, 1994.
4. Letter from Marty Kalb to author, Mar. 18, 1994.
5. For Zimiles see letter to author, Mar. 17, 1994. For Oransky see letter to author Mar. 21, 1994. For Bialobroda see letter to author, Mar. 14, 1995. For Witkin see letter to author, Mar. 25, 1994.
6. Letter from Sidney Chafetz to author, Dec. 12, 1995; and *Perpetrators* (Upper Arlington, Ohio: Upper Arlington Municipal Center, 1991, 1995).
7. For Graupe-Pillard see letter to author, Apr. 14, 1996. For Erony see letter to author, Aug. 1, 1995.
8. Young, *Writing and Rewriting the Holocaust*, 100, 102, 103.

Expressing the Inexpressible

1. "Artist's Statement," *Perpetrators*, 9.
2. Letter from Arnold Trachtman to author, May 30, 1995; "Statement," *Witness and Legacy*, 44; and Peter J. Baldaia, *Approaching a Horrible Truth Through Art: Two Artists Painting the Holocaust, Arnold Trachtman and Susan Erony* (Newtonville, Mass.: Newton Arts Center, 1992), n.p.
3. Typed statements about the film and the video; letter from Eleanor Antin to the author, Apr. 4, 1994; *From the Inside Out: Eight Contemporary Artists* (New York: Jewish Museum, 1993), 24–25. For Thomas Hart Benton, see Baigell, "Benton and the Left," 1–34.
4. Helen Fein, *Accounting for Genocide* (New York: The Free Press, 1979), cited in Michael Berenbaum, "The Nativization of the Holocaust," *Judaism* 35 (Fall 1986): 456.
5. Letter from Judith Goldstein to author, Feb. 2, 1996.
6. Letters from Louise Kramer to author, Apr. 12, 1996, and May 1, 1996.
7. Joan Simon, "An Interview with Jonathan Borofsky," *Art in America* 69 (Mar. 1981): 162–166; Mark Rosenthal, "Jonathan Borofsky's Modes of Working," in Mark Rosenthal and Richard Marshall, eds., *Jonathan Borofsky* (New York: Harry N. Abrams, 1984), 19; and Amishai-Maisels, *Depiction and Interpretation*, 332–333.
8. *Jewish Themes/Contemporary Artists II*, 8; Frank, *Hannelore Baron: Collages and Box Constructions*, 17.

9. Letter to author, Mar. 3, 1996; Ori Z. Soltes, *Intimations of Immortality: The Paintings of Kitty Klaidman and Elyse Klaidman* (Washington, D.C.: B'nai B'rith Klutznick National Jewish Museum, 1994): 2–14; statement in Bohm-Duchen, *After Auschwitz*, 150; statement in Feinstein, ed., *Witness and Legacy*, 35.

10. This information is based on several years of conversations with the artist.

11. Soltes, *Intimations of Immortality: The Paintings of Kitty Klaidman and Elyse Klaidman*, 26.

12. Letters to author, Jan. 29 and July 17, 1995; *Witness and Legacy*, 45; *St. Paul Pioneer Press*, sect. E, 1.

13. Kuppermann, "'The Far Country': A Photographic Journey," 1994; statement for "Installation: The Far Country," 1995.

14. Letters to author, Oct. 13, 1995, and May 21, 1996; statement, Bohm-Duchen, *After Auschwitz*, 148.

15. Rose, *From Ashes to the Rainbow*, 15–19.

16. Statement in *Political Visions: Gerda Meyer-Bernstein, Installationen und Objekte* (Berlin: Neuer Berliner Kunstverein, 1987), n.p.; artist's statement, *Gerda Meyer-Bernstein* (Chicago: Beacon Street Gallery, 1993), n.p.; Cindy Kranz, "Grim Reminders," *Rockford Register Star*, Sept. 5, 1991.

17. Claude Lanzmann, *Shoah: An Oral History of the Holocaust* (New York: Pantheon Books, 1985), 104; and letter to author, Apr. 18, 1996.

18. Langer, *Holocaust Testimonies*, 54, 55–56.

19. Letter to author, Mar. 21, 1994.

20. Langer, *Admitting the Holocaust*, 8.

21. Letter to author, Mar. 3, 1995.

22. Letter to author, Feb. 10, 1996.

23. For Stein see statement, "Never Again."

24. Letters to author, Jan. 12, 1994, and Mar. 18, 1994.

25. Aharon Appelfeld, "After the Holocaust," in Beral Lang, ed., *Writing and the Holocaust* (New York: Holmes and Meier, 1998), 92, cited in Langer, *Admitting the Holocaust*, 182. See also Waldi, *Memorial Candles: Children of the Holocaust*, 7–8, 15.

26. Statement, "Never Again"; statement for Robert Mann Gallery, New York, n.d.; letter to author, Oct. 26, 1995.

27. Roland Barthes, *Camera Lucida*, trans. Richard Howard (New York: Hill & Wang, 1981), 82.

28. Chayat, *Life Lessons*, 25–27, 68; letter to author, Mar. 25, 1994; unpublished interview, Nov. 4, 1991.

29. Andreas Huyssen, "Monument and Memory in a Post Modern Age," in Young, *The Art of Memory*, 16.

30. Langer, *Admitting the Holocaust*, 103–104, 20.

31. Letters to author, May 30, 1992, Mar. 27, 1994, May 5, 1995, Oct. 17, 1995; Stephen Feinstein, "Pearl Hirshfield—Expanding the Boundaries of Art and Politics," in *Pearl Hirshfield* (River Falls: University of Wisconsin, 1995); 6; and material furnished by the artist.

32. Letter to author, May 21, 1996.

33. Letter to author, May 24, 1996. See Elie Weisel, *Night*, trans. Stella Rodway (New York: Bantam Books, 1986), 95–96.

34. Kuspit, "The Abandoned Nude," *Natan Nuchi*, n.p.; statement, Aug. 1944; from an English typescript of an article (in Hebrew) by Michael Sgan-Cohen "'Yellow Star at Night' The Paintings of Natan Nuchi, an interview by Haim Maor," *Studio* (Dec. 1990). Parts of the interview are reprinted in *Natan Nuchi* (Haifa: Museum of Modern Art, 1992), 55–64.

35. Audrey Flack, *On Painting* (New York: Harry N. Abrams, 1981), 20, 78, 81; typed memorandum, Jewish Museum Files; John Perrault, "Audrey Flack—Odds Against the House," *Soho Weekly News* (Mar. 23, 1978): 20, cited in Amishai-Maisels, *Depiction and Interpretation*, 17; Laurence Alloway, *Audrey Flack— Vanitas* (New York: Louis K. Meisel Gallery, 1978), n.p.; taped conversation with author, Apr. 30, 1992; Rittner and Roth, *Different Voices*, 81, 384.

36. Letter to author, Sept. 19, 1995; Young, *The Texture of Memory*, 17–19.

37. Letter to author, Feb. 11, 1996.

38. Artist's statement, Jan. 1995; several telephone conversations with the artist over a period of years.

39. *Grace Graupe-Pillard: Nowhere to Go and The Holocaust Series* (Trenton: New Jersey State Museum, 1993); letter to author, Apr. 13, 1996.

40. Letters to author, July 18 and May 4, 1996; Gabrielle Rossmer, "In Search of the Lost Object," pamphlet, n.d.

41. Andrea Liss "(Im)Possible Evidence," in *Impossible Evidence: Contemporary Artists View the Holocaust* (Reading, Pa.: Freedman Gallery, Albright College, 1994), 14.

42. Elizabeth A. Brown, "Reading The Anne Frank Project," *The Anne Frank Project* (Santa Barbara: University Art Museum, University of California, 1993), 9. Discussion of the installation is based on this essay. See also statement, Bohm-Duchen, *After Auschwitz*, 155.

43. For Rivers's portraits, see Sam Hunter, *Larry Rivers* (New York: Rizzoli, 1989), 53, 184, 185, 339.

44. *The Holocaust in Contemporary Art*, n.p.; *From Inside Out*, 34, 35, 44; Bohm-Duchen, *After Auschwitz*, 156; *Impossible Evidence*, 25, 27.

45. Letter to author, Dec. 22, 1992.

46. Rosenfeld, *A Double Dying*, 160, 27.

47. Judy Chicago, *Holocaust Project: From Darkness to Light* (New York: Penguin Books, 1993), 9.

48. Statement in *Political Visions*, n.p.

49. *Holocaust Project Newsletter* 3 (Summer 1989), n.p. For the panels, see Chicago, *Holocaust Project*, plates 9, 18.

50. *Jewish Themes/Contemporary American Artists II*, 44. See also Susan Jacobowitz, "A Conversation with Art Spiegelman," *Artweek* 24 (Dec. 16, 1993): 16; Matthew Friedman, "When It's a Matter of Life and Death," *Arts Magazine* 65 (Oct. 1990): 83; Art Spiegelman, *Maus* (New York: Pantheon Books, 1986). *Maus II* was published in 1991.

51. Letter to author, June 18, 1995.

52. Statement that is part of video presentation, May 1990; letter to author, Nov. 14, 1993; Ann Poore " 'Jew' Exhibit Recalls Holocaust," *Salt Lake City Tribune,* Apr. 7, 1991, sec. E, 1.
53. Letter to author, Mar. 4, 1996.
54. Letters to author, Apr. 23 and May 16, 1996.
55. Jacob, "The Artist in Society," 2–6; exhibition statement, "Reclaiming the Symbol/The Art of Memory."
56. Chayat, *Life Lessons,* 68.
57. Letter to author, June 6, 1995.
58. Chayat, *Life Lessons,* 69.
59. Michael Wyschograd, "Some Theological Reflections on the Holocaust," in Steinitz with Szonyi, *Living After the Holocaust,* 68.
60. Theodor Adorno, "Cultural Criticism and Society," *Prisms,* trans. Samuel and Shierry Weber (Cambridge, Mass.: MIT Press, 1981), 34; and *Negative Dialectics* (1966), trans. E. B. Ashton (New York: Seabury Press, 1973), 362.
61. *Murray Zimiles: The Fire Paintings, The Book of Fire,* n.p.
62. Kuppermann, "A Far Country: A Photographic Journey."
63. Sgan-Cohen, "Touching the Essence: The Work of Natan Nuchi," 63–64.
64. *Salt Lake City Tribune,* Apr. 7, 1991, sec. E, 1.

INDEX

ABOUT THE AUTHOR

Matthew Baigell, who holds the rank of Professor II in Rutgers University's art history department, is a specialist in American art. He has written *A Thomas Hart Benton Miscellany* (editor), *A History of American Painting, Thomas Hart Benton, The American Scene: American Painting During the 1930s, Charles Burchfield, Frederic Remington, Dictionary of American Art, Thomas Cole, Albert Bierstadt, A Concise History of American Painting and Sculpture, Artists Against War and Fascism: The Papers of the First American Artists' Congress* (coeditor), and *Soviet Dissident Art: Interviews after Perestroika* (coauthor), and dozens of articles as well as essays for exhibition catalogs. He is currently engaged in research for a book on Ralph Waldo Emerson's presence in twentieth-century American art.